OUR WORLD

INCREDIBLE BUT TRUE FACTS

This edition published by Parragon Books Ltd in 2015

Parragon Books Ltd
Chartist House
15–17 Trim Street
Bath BA1 1HA, UK
www.parragon.com

Copyright © Parragon Books Ltd 2008-2015

Written by Jen Green
Consultant: John Williams

ISBN 978-1-4748-1410-2

Printed in China

OUR WORLD
INCREDIBLE BUT
TRUE FACTS

PaRragon

Bath · New York · Cologne · Melbourne · Delhi
Hong Kong · Shenzhen · Singapore · Amsterdam

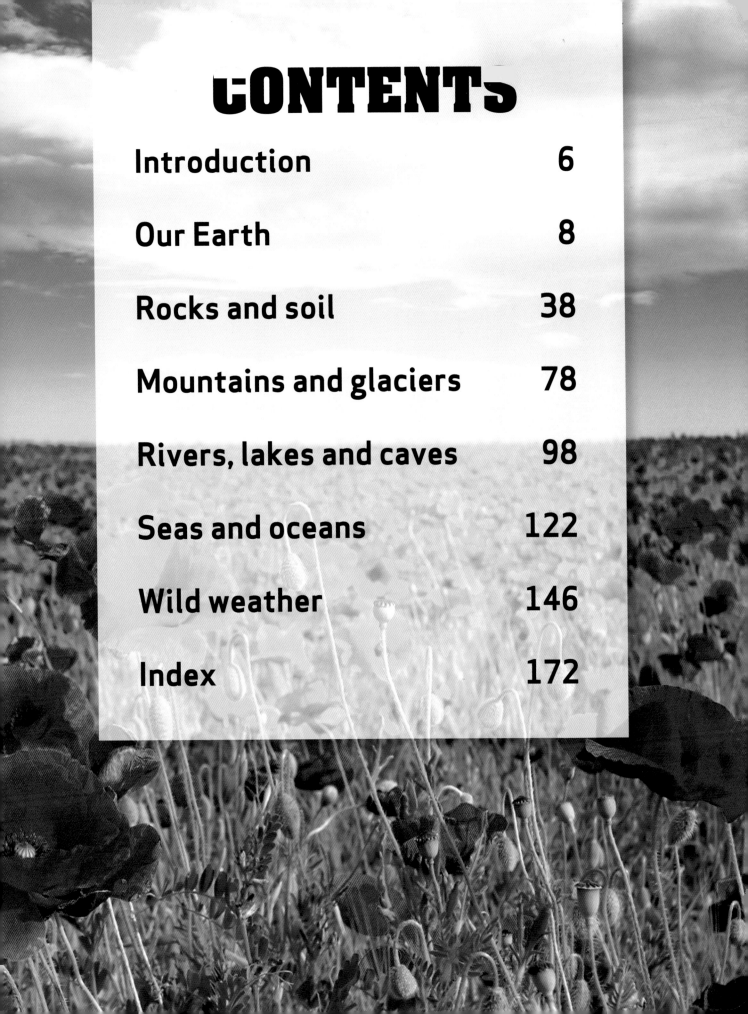

CONTENTS

Introduction

From space, the Earth looks like a big blue ball with white clouds drifting over it. Our world has just the right conditions for plant and animal life to survive. The Sun lights and warms the Earth. Water fills the rivers and oceans, and the air contains a gas called oxygen, which animals need to breathe.

This book explains all about the Earth, its rocks and soil, mountains, valleys, rivers and oceans. You can find out about earthquakes and volcanoes, and also learn about the different kinds of weather on our planet.

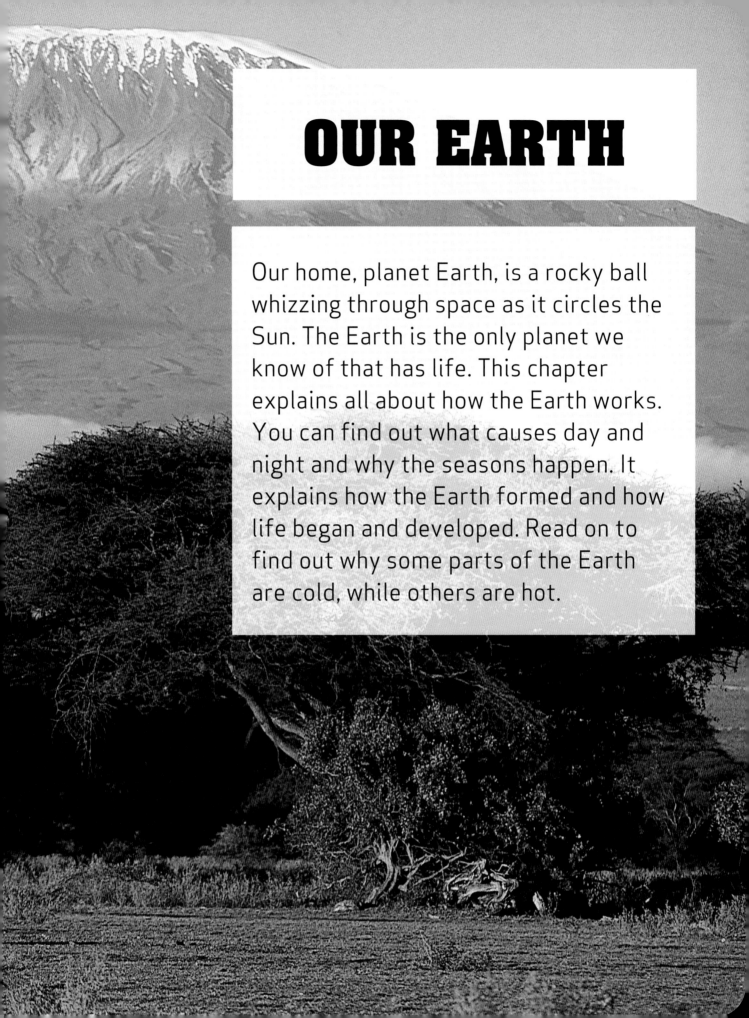

OUR EARTH

Our home, planet Earth, is a rocky ball whizzing through space as it circles the Sun. The Earth is the only planet we know of that has life. This chapter explains all about how the Earth works. You can find out what causes day and night and why the seasons happen. It explains how the Earth formed and how life began and developed. Read on to find out why some parts of the Earth are cold, while others are hot.

Our Solar System

The Earth is one of eight main planets circling the Sun. The Sun, these planets and a number of dwarf planets and smaller rocks make up the solar system. As they circle the Sun, the Earth and the planets follow paths called orbits.

The planets

The Earth is the third planet from the Sun, after Mercury and Venus. The Earth is the fifth-biggest planet, but all the planets are tiny compared to the Sun.

Sun

 Mercury

 Venus

 Earth

 Mars

Jupiter

The Sun

The Sun is our local star. It is an enormous fiery ball shooting light and heat in all directions. The Sun's rays light and heat the Earth. Without the Sun's warmth and energy, almost no living things could survive on the Earth.

North Pole

The Earth

The Earth looks blue from space because it is mainly covered by oceans. The Equator is an imaginary line that divides the Earth into two halves called hemispheres. The Poles are the places furthest north and south on the Earth.

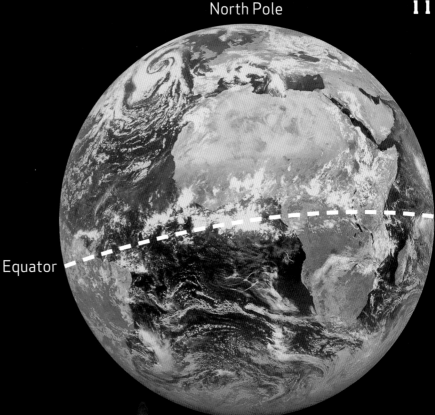

Equator

South Pole

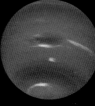

Pluto
(dwarf planet)

Saturn

Uranus

Neptune

Stars

All the stars in the night sky are suns, like our Sun. Believe it or not, our Sun is just one of 100 billion stars in our part of the universe. Our Sun belongs to a huge group of stars called the Milky Way.

Spinning Earth

The Earth seems still but, in fact, our world is spinning as it circles the Sun. This spin is called rotation. It takes 24 hours to complete one full rotation, which we call a day.

Day and night

The Earth rotates around an imaginary line called the axis, which joins the North and South Poles. When the Earth turns into the sunlight, it is day where you live. When the Earth turns out of the sunlight, it is night.

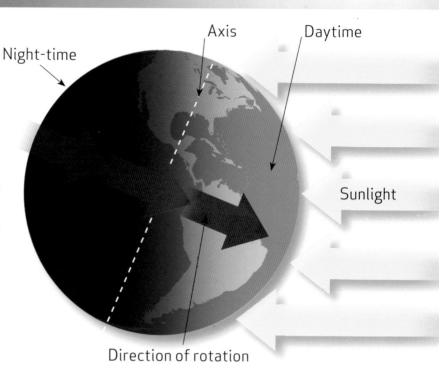

Night-time

Axis

Daytime

Sunlight

Direction of rotation

Daytime

When the day begins, the Sun seems to rise in the east. It then moves across the sky and goes down, or sets, in the west. But the Sun isn't really moving. The Earth's rotation produces this effect.

When an object blocks the sunlight, it makes a shadow. When you wave, your shadow waves too!

Night-time

When it is dark, your part of the Earth faces away from the Sun. The Moon and stars shine in the darkness. The Moon has no light of its own but is lit up by the Sun.

Did you know?

The Sun is about 150 million kilometres from the Earth. It takes just over eight minutes for sunlight to reach the Earth. Light travels at about 300,000 kilometres per second.

Night owls

Many people and animals are awake and busy during the day when the Sun shines and we can see clearly. Most of us sleep at night when it's dark and we can't see much, but some animals, such as owls, hunt at night.

The owl's large eyes help it to hunt in dim light at dusk or by moonlight.

The Earth's Orbit

As you sit still reading this, the Earth is racing on its journey, or orbit, around the Sun. It takes 365 days to complete one full orbit. We call this a year. The Earth tilts, and this produces the regular changes we call the seasons.

The Earth's tilt

The Earth leans over as it rotates and orbits the Sun. This tilt carries places on the Earth nearer to or further from the Sun at different times of the year.

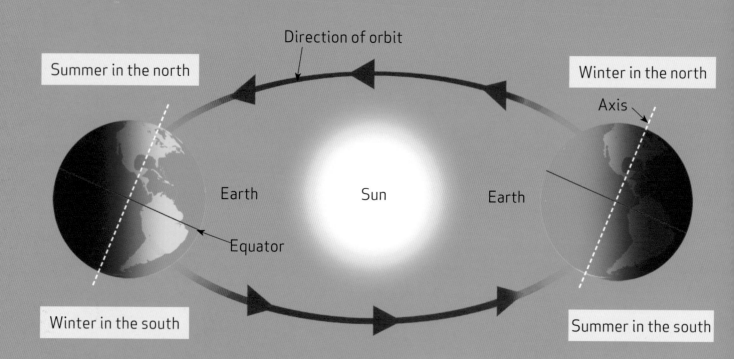

Direction of orbit

Summer in the north

Winter in the north

Axis

Earth

Sun

Earth

Equator

Winter in the south

Summer in the south

The seasons

As the Earth orbits the Sun, the northern half of the world leans towards the Sun and has summer. The southern half leans away and has winter. Six months later, the northern half is leaning away from the Sun, and the seasons are reversed.

Did you know?

The seasons are most noticeable at the Poles. This is because these parts are most affected by the Earth's tilt.

Daffodils are spring flowers.

Spring

In spring, your part of the Earth starts to lean towards the Sun. The days get longer and the weather warms up. Flowers bloom and trees grow new leaves.

Summer

Days are long and nights are short in summer. Your part of the Earth tilts towards the Sun. This is the hottest season.

Autumn

In autumn, your part of the Earth begins to lean away from the Sun. Days get shorter and nights get longer. The weather grows colder.

In autumn, some leaves change colour and fall off the trees.

Winter

Winter brings long nights and short days. This is the coldest season. The part of the Earth where you live is tilted away from the Sun.

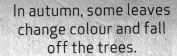

The Atmosphere

The Earth is wrapped in a protective blanket of gases called the atmosphere. This blanket makes life possible on the Earth. Our weather is created in the lowest layer.

Atmosphere stretches about 800 km above the Earth's surface. Beyond is space.

Exosphere (stretches out into space)

Thermosphere (up to 700 kilometres)

Mesosphere (up to 100 kilometres)

Blanket of gases

The main atmosphere gases are nitrogen and oxygen, which is vital for life. Small amounts of other gases help to trap the Sun's heat and filter out harmful rays. The Earth's gravity keeps the atmosphere in place.

Layers of atmosphere

The atmosphere has five layers stacked on top of one another. The lowest, the troposphere, contains 75 per cent of the atmosphere's gases. The air thins out as you head towards the exosphere and space.

Stratosphere (up to 50 kilometres)

Troposphere (up to 10 kilometres)

Thin air

The higher you go, the less oxygen there is. Mountaineers use bottled oxygen in the 'thin air' to help them breathe. The air on the highest mountains contains about one-third of the gases found at sea level.

Above the clouds

Clouds form in the lowest layer of the atmosphere. Planes can climb to the next layer, the stratosphere, to get above the clouds and avoid storms.

Top of cloud cover

Did you know?

The Earth's atmosphere helps to protect us from meteors (rocks falling from space). Meteors usually burn up high in the atmosphere, to form 'shooting stars'.

Forces on the Earth

The Earth's huge size and weight make it pull objects towards it. This pull, called gravity, prevents you and everything else on the Earth from flying off into space!

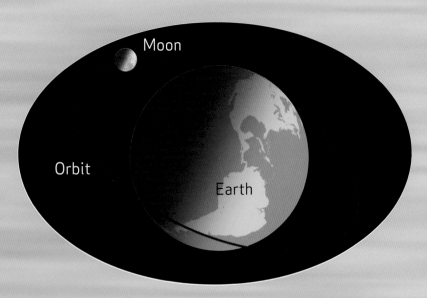

Moon

Orbit

Earth

The Moon

The Earth's gravity keeps the Moon orbiting around it. The Moon also has gravity, which tugs at the oceans on the Earth.

Gravity

The Earth's gravity causes anything you drop to fall to the ground. All objects have gravity. Large, heavy objects such as planets have the most gravity. The Sun's gravity is very strong. It keeps the Earth and other planets in the solar system rotating around it.

Did you know?

The area affected by a planet's magnetic pull is called its magnetic field. The Earth's magnetic field stretches 60,000 kilometres into space.

Magnetic pull

Scientists believe that iron inside the Earth makes it magnetic – it acts like a giant bar magnet. The ends of this magnet are near the North and South Poles. The Earth's magnetic pull reaches far out into space.

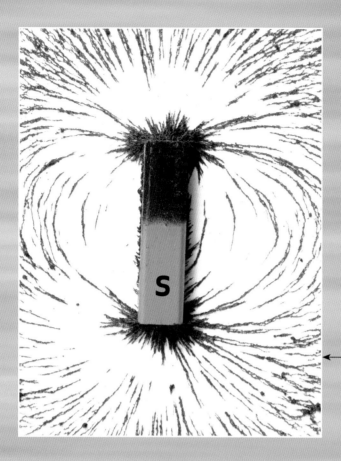

← Tiny pieces of iron called filings are pulled towards this bar magnet, showing its magnetic field.

Which way is north?

The Earth's North and South Poles have a very strong magnetic pull. A compass contains a magnetic needle that points to the north. It can be used to help people find their way if they are lost.

However high you jump on a trampoline, the pull of gravity will bring you back to the Earth!

← The Sun

How the Earth Formed

The Earth is incredibly old. Scientists believe the Sun and planets began to form about five billion years ago. Our solar system developed from a cloud of gas and dust spinning in space.

The solar system forms

Gas in the centre of the spinning cloud formed the Sun. Bits of dust stuck together to make rocks. These crashed and stuck together to make rocky planets, including the Earth. Meanwhile, the Sun's gravity kept the planets rotating around it.

Pieces of rock orbiting the Sun crashed together to form larger rocks and planets.

Early Earth

The young planet Earth was a fiery ball of hot, liquid rock. The heat came from all the rocks that had crashed together. Heavy rocks sank to the planet's centre. Lighter rocks floated to the surface. There, they gradually cooled to make a crust.

Rocks from space

The early Earth had no atmosphere to shield it from space.
Giant rocks called meteorites crashed to the planet's surface.
They made large hollows called craters.

Meteorite crater,
Arizona, United States

The Earth facts

- The Earth's inside is still red-hot, liquid rock. The outside has cooled and hardened to make a solid crust.
- The Earth is not perfectly round. It bulges slightly in the middle and is flatter at the Poles.
- The Earth is tiny compared to the Sun. You could fit more than a million Earths inside the Sun.

Volcanoes everywhere

About four billion years ago, the Earth's surface was dotted with volcanoes (see pages 66–71) erupting red-hot melted rock, or lava. Gas and steam from the volcanoes formed the Earth's first atmosphere. The steam formed clouds, which dropped rain. The water collected in hollows, which eventually became the oceans.

Life Begins and Changes

Scientists believe that life began on the Earth about 3.8 billion years ago. Over millions of years, living things very slowly changed to suit their surroundings. These changes are called evolution.

First life

The first living things appeared in the oceans. They were tiny, simple creatures called bacteria, made of just one cell. Much later, tiny plants called algae developed in the sea.

Plants make oxygen

The algae used the Sun's energy to grow. They gave off oxygen. Some of these tiny plants grew in mounds called stromatolites. These mounds still grow in warm seas today.

Stromatolite mounds, Australia

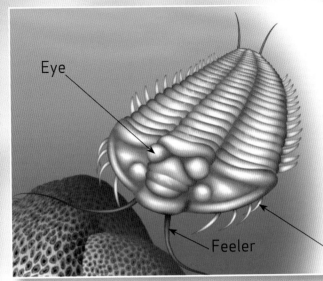

Eye

Feeler

Animals appear

The first animals appeared in the oceans about 600 million years ago. They were very simple creatures, with soft bodies. Gradually, animals developed more complicated bodies made up of many cells. Some, such as sea creatures called trilobites, developed hard shells.

Trilobites had many legs.

Life moves onto land

About 400 million years ago, the first animals with backbones appeared. They were fish. Gradually, many different types of fish evolved. Some developed fleshy fins and crawled out of the water to live on land.

Mudskippers are fish that can move about on land.

Did you know?

Trilobites were among the first animals with eyes that saw the world clearly. They also had feelers on their heads, which they used to search for food.

Fossils

Fossils are the remains of plants and animals that lived and died millions of years ago. The remains have been preserved, usually as rock. Scientists discover all about prehistoric life by studying fossils.

This is a fossil of an ammonite. The hard shell of this ammonite has turned to rock.

Ammonite

Ammonites were creatures that swam in the oceans millions of years ago. The living animal had tentacles that stuck out of its coiled shell.

How ammonite fossils formed

When the ammonite died, it sank to the seabed. The soft parts rotted away, and the shell was buried by sand. Over millions of years, the sand slowly hardened into rock. Minerals seeped into the shell, until it too became rock.

Dead ammonite sank to the seabed.

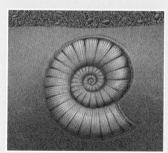

Ammonite and sand slowly turned to rock.

Amber

Amber is a different kind of fossil. The clear, yellow material is fossilized tree resin – a sticky sap that oozed from prehistoric trees. Insects got trapped in the sap, which then hardened to make a fossil.

You can see the insects' delicate legs and wings in this fossil.

Amber fossils may be up to 90 million years old.

Fossil fern

The print of a fern leaf has been preserved in this rock. Ferns like warm, damp conditions. They grew well in the steamy prehistoric forests 300 million years ago.

Prehistoric Life

Since life began, many amazing animals have lived on the Earth. We call the long period from 230 million years ago to 65 million years ago the Age of Reptiles. During this time, giant reptiles ruled the land, sky and sea.

Tyrannosaurus Rex was a fierce meat-eating dinosaur.

Dinosaurs

A group of reptiles called the dinosaurs roamed the land. There were many sorts of dinosaurs. Some were only as big as cats. Others were bigger than a house. Some dinosaurs were meat eaters, while others ate only plants.

Did you know?

The largest dinosaurs measured about 33 metres long. The ground shook when they walked. The very biggest dinosaurs were plant eaters. There are no dinosaurs living today.

Plesiosaurs swam using their feet as paddles.

Swimming and flying reptiles

Other huge reptiles swam in the oceans. Plesiosaurs had long, snake-like necks and feet shaped like paddles. Another group of reptiles, the pterosaurs, soared through the skies on skin-covered wings.

Dinosaur fossils

This scientist is uncovering the skeleton of a dinosaur. He is chipping away the rock to reveal the fossil. Dinosaur bones have been found all over the world. Experts also find dinosaur tracks, and even dinosaur dung.

Dinosaurs die out

The dinosaurs and other giant reptiles died out around 65 million years ago. Experts believe a giant space rock, or meteorite, smashed into the Earth, causing a huge dust cloud to block the Sun for years. As a result, many plants died and there was not enough food for the dinosaurs.

The meteorite exploded when it hit the Earth. The disaster made the Earth's climate change suddenly.

The Earth's Climate

Climate is the regular pattern of weather. Each part of the Earth has its own climate. The Sun has a big effect on the climate, but so do mountains, the seas and the cities.

Heat from the Sun

The Sun's rays are directly overhead at the Equator. This region has a hot, tropical climate. At the Poles, the Sun's rays spread over a wider area, so they have less heating power. This means that the Poles have a cold climate.

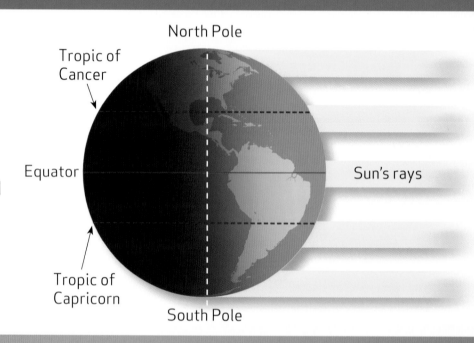

North Pole

Tropic of Cancer

Equator

Sun's rays

Tropic of Capricorn

South Pole

Did you know?

The sea warms up and cools down more slowly than the land, keeping temperatures on the coast steady. Many places far inland have very hot summers and very cold winters because they are far from the sea.

Coastal climates

Many places by the sea have a mild climate. Temperatures stay fairly steady there because sea breezes cool the land in summer and warm it in winter.

Cool heights

Mountains usually have a cold climate. The air high on mountains cannot hold as much of the Sun's heat as the air at sea level. The tops of high mountains are covered with ice and snow all year round.

Clouds bring rain to mountains.

City climates

Cities only cover quite a small area of the planet but have their own climate. Buildings and roads soak up the Sun's heat by day and give it out at night. This makes cities warmer than the nearby countryside.

Climate Zones

A region's climate affects the plants and animals that live there. Large areas of the Earth's surface have the same types of plants growing there. These regions are called biomes.

The Earth's biomes

You can see the world's main biomes on this map. The types of plants that grow in each place depend on how warm it is and how much rain falls. Hot, rainy places have many types of plants. Fewer plants grow in cold or dry places.

THE ARCT

NORTH AMERICA

SOUTH AMERICA

Key to biomes

- Mountains
- Tropical rainforests
- Temperate woodlands
- Evergreen forests
- Tropical grasslands
- Temperate grasslands
- Tundra
- Deserts
- Polar regions

Deserts

Deserts are very dry places where less than 25 centimetres of rain falls each year. Some deserts get no rain at all for years. Deserts may be sandy, rocky or stony. Many are boiling hot by day and freezing cold at night.

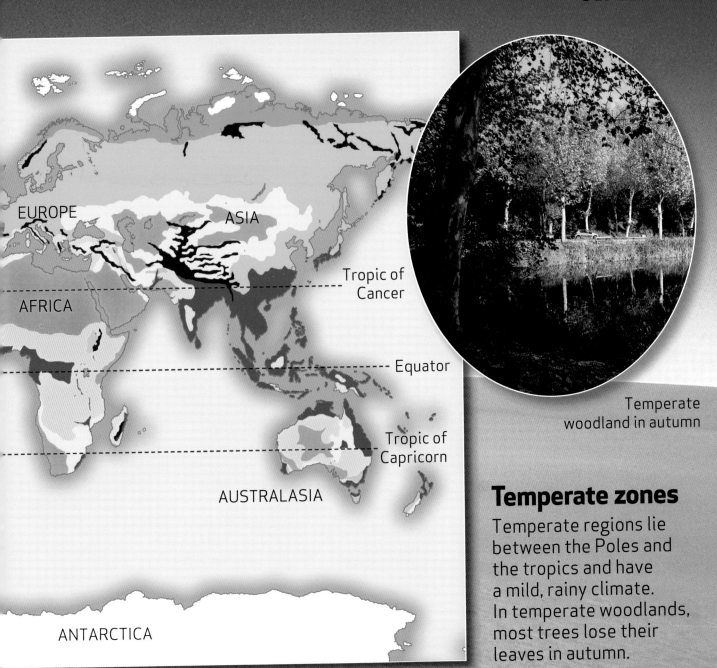

EUROPE

ASIA

Tropic of
Cancer

AFRICA

Equator

Tropic of
Capricorn

AUSTRALASIA

ANTARCTICA

Temperate
woodland in autumn

Temperate zones

Temperate regions lie
between the Poles and
the tropics and have
a mild, rainy climate.
In temperate woodlands,
most trees lose their
leaves in autumn.

Cold forests
and tundra

In the cold northern forests,
trees stay green all year. Little
grows in the icy tundra except
during the short summer.
The ground beneath the surface
stays frozen all year.

Plants bloom during
the short tundra summer.

The Water Cycle

Moisture moves between the air, oceans and land in a never-ending cycle. As the water moves around, it changes from a liquid into a gas and back again.

Sun

Powered by the Sun

The Sun powers the water cycle by warming the air. Warm air holds more moisture than cold air. When warm, moist air cools, clouds form and bring rain.

2. Warm, moist air blows inland.

1. Moisture rises into the air.

5. Rivers drain into the sea.

Rising moisture

As the Sun warms the sea, moisture rises into the air in the form of a gas called water vapour. This process is known as evaporation. Winds blow the warm, moist air towards the land.

3. Clouds form as warm air rises and cools.

4. Rain falls from clouds and runs into rivers.

Clouds form

When warm, moist air rises over hills or mountains, it cools. The water vapour turns into tiny drops of water or ice, which gather to make clouds. The clouds bring rain, snow or hail.

Did you know?

The rain that falls where you live has fallen many times before in other places. No new water forms on the Earth – it is just recycled naturally.

Soaking up water

When it rains, some water drains into rivers and travels back to the sea. Rainwater also soaks into the ground. Trees draw up moisture through their roots and release it through their leaves.

Places on the Equator and in the tropics have hot climates. It is warm there all year round, and nights are never frosty. Snow only falls on the tops of the very highest mountains.

Death Valley is a desert valley in the western United States.

Hottest places

Dallol in East Africa has the hottest average temperature on the planet – it stays at about 34 degrees Celsius. Death Valley, United States, has some of the highest temperatures – up to 56 degrees Celsius – but it does not stay that hot all year round.

Two seasons

The climate in the tropics is not affected by the Earth's tilt, so there is no spring, summer, autumn or winter. But some tropical places have two seasons: a dry and a rainy season.

India has its wet season from April to September every year.

Lush rainforests

Rain falls almost every day on most places at the Equator. Rainforest trees love the hot, damp conditions. More types of plants and animals live in tropical rainforests than in any other biome.

Did you know?

In 1913, one part of Death Valley had the highest temperature ever recorded on the Earth. It was 56.7 degrees Celsius.

Hot grasslands

Tropical grasslands grow in places that get less rain than rainforests but more rain than deserts. These areas are home to many grass-eating animals, such as zebras and antelopes, and the animals that feed on them, such as lions.

Lions live on the tropical grasslands in Africa.

The Sun shines all
night in summer at the Poles.

Cold Climates

The regions surrounding the North and
South Poles are the coldest places on
the Earth. The Sun's rays have little
warmth there. Most land in the polar
regions is covered by a thick layer of
ice and snow.

Midnight sun

In summer, each Pole tilts towards
the Sun. At night, the Sun dips low in
the sky, but never sets. So it stays
light, even at midnight. In winter,
the Pole leans away from the
Sun. The Sun never fully
rises, so it is dark all
the time.

Shimmering lights

Swirling curtains of light
sometimes shimmer in the night
sky at the Poles. These beautiful
lights are called auroras. The lights
may be red, green or purple. This
amazing display is caused by
particles from the Sun hitting
gases high in the air.

The Arctic

The area around
the North Pole is
called the Arctic.
This region is mainly
an ice-covered ocean.
Polar bears and seals live
in the sea and on the ice.

This polar bear is
hunting seals on the ice.

Did you know?

Vostok Station in
Antarctica is the
coldest place on
the Earth. Scientists
recorded a
temperature of
−89 degrees
Celsius there.

Penguins have thick
feathers and a
warm, fatty layer
under their skin.

Antarctica

The area around the South Pole is called
the Antarctic. The vast icy land of
Antarctica lies in this area. Antarctica is
covered with a thick cap of ice up to four
kilometres deep. No animals live inland,
but penguins and seals live on the coast.

ROCKS AND SOIL

This chapter explains how rocks form and how the rocks at the surface are broken down by rain, wind, frost and sunlight. Underground there are many riches, such as gold, silver and diamonds. Valuable fossil fuels – coal, oil and gas – come from beneath the ground too. But soil, which lies on top of the Earth's rocky surface, may be the greatest treasure of all. Read on to find out why.

Rocky Planet

We live on the Earth's hard, rocky surface called the crust. Deep below the crust, the rocks are hot – so hot they are melted and flow like sticky treacle.

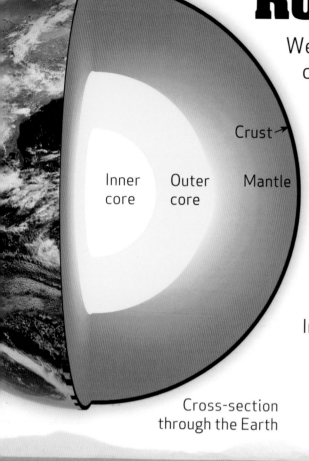

Crust

Inner core   Outer core   Mantle

Cross-section through the Earth

Inside the Earth

Scientists believe the Earth is made of several layers. The surface crust is thin. Below the crust is a thick layer called the mantle, with red-hot rocks. In the core at the centre, the rocks are hotter still.

The Earth's rocky crust at the Grand Canyon, United States

Heat from below

Deep mines are hot because of the hot rocks below. But even the very deepest mines are just like a pinprick in the giant rocky ball that is the Earth.

This man is working in a hot, deep mine.

Thin crust

Ocean

Land

Thick crust

Rocky crust

Cliffs and mountains are formed from the Earth's crust. If you stripped away the grass, soil or concrete at any place on the Earth, you'd hit rock. These cliffs were made by a river cutting through the rock.

Ocean crust

The Earth's crust is thicker beneath the land than beneath the oceans. The crust beneath the land is 20 to 90 kilometres thick. Beneath the oceans, it is only about seven kilometres thick.

Did you know?

Scientists believe the temperature at the centre of the Earth is around 6000 degrees Celsius. The outer core is made of partly liquid rock. The inner core is a solid ball of metal.

Fiery Rocks

Rocks form in different ways. Fiery rocks come from deep underground. Red-hot, liquid rock bubbles up to near the surface, then cools to form solid rock.

Glowing lava

Red-hot, liquid rock deep underground is called magma. When it spills on to the surface at a volcano (see pages 66–71), it is called lava. Lava cools and hardens quickly at the surface.

Frothy pumice

A type of rock called pumice was once frothy lava. Like froth on a fizzy drink, it contains air bubbles. The bubbles were trapped when the lava cooled. Bubbles make this rock so light it floats on water.

People use pumice to rub away hard skin while bathing.

Six-sided basalt pillars

Giant's Causeway

Basalt is a hard fiery rock. Volcanoes on the seabed erupt melted basalt. The red-hot lava cools quickly when it hits the water. The Giant's Causeway in Northern Ireland is made of basalt pillars. These formed when the lava cooled quickly, shrank and cracked.

Did you know?

The rocky pillars at the Giant's Causeway mainly have six sides. Legend says a giant laid the rocks as stepping stones.

A granite building in Scotland

Granite

Granite is another hard fiery rock. It forms where magma rises but cools before it reaches the surface. This hard stone is used for making buildings and roads.

Wearing Away

The rocks at the surface are battered by rain, wind, frost and sunshine. Bits of rock flake off and are carried away by wind and water. This process is called erosion.

Did you know?
Erosion usually happens quite slowly. But sometimes a large amount of rock slips away at once. This is called a landslide.

This flat slab of limestone is criss-crossed with deep grooves.

Eating into rock

Rainwater contains a weak acid that eats into soft rocks such as limestone. This is similar to when an aspirin dissolves in water. The rainwater slowly wears deep grooves in the rock.

Shattered by ice

In cold places, such as on mountainsides, water seeps into cracks in the rock and freezes at night. Ice takes up more space than water, so the ice widens the cracks. Eventually, the rock flakes away.

Ice has made this rock crack.

Worn by wind

In dry, windy places, sand and grit are carried on the wind. When the wind blasts against rock, the sand and grit act like sandpaper. This can carve smooth curves into the rock.

This rock in Western Australia is called Wave Rock.

Carried away

When it rains, trickling water carries away small pieces of loose rock. The water drains into streams and rivers, which carry the rocky pieces downhill. They end up in seas or lakes.

Settled-down Rocks

Fiery rocks are not the only type of rock. Another type forms from rocky pieces that are carried out to sea by rivers. The pieces are squashed together by more rocky fragments and eventually turn into solid rock.

Rock layers

When the rocky pieces are carried out to sea, they settle in layers on the seabed. Later, the rock layers may be pushed upwards when mountains form (see pages 82–83) and become part of the land.

You can see the rock layers in this sandstone cliff in New Zealand.

Clay pots

Clay is a rock that is soft when wet. Potters shape clay to make pots. The pots are baked in an oven to make them hard.

These children are helping to make a clay pot.

Puddingstone

A rock called conglomerate contains round pebbles that settled on the seabed. When the layer was squashed, the pebbles stuck together. The rock is also sometimes called puddingstone because it looks like pudding mixture.

These cliffs are made of chalk.

Did you know?

Fossils, the remains of ancient plants and animals, are often found in layered rocks, such as sandstone and limestone.

Chalk

Chalk is a soft, white rock made of the tiny shells of millions of sea creatures. The shells built up on the seabed and were later buried. The shell layer very slowly turned to chalk. This rock can be used to draw on blackboards and pavements.

Changed Rocks

Changed rocks are another type of rock. They form when rocks are heated or squeezed below ground. The rocks may be squeezed by other rocks on top of them, or they may be squeezed by magma rising upwards, which can also heat the rock.

Did you know?

Marble is a changed rock. Some of the world's most famous sculptures have been carved from this rock.

Heated rock

This is a changed rock called gneiss. The wavy lines show where the rock layers have been melted and squeezed. Sometimes squeezing happens when rocks shift underground during earthquakes (see pages 72–77).

Slate

Slate forms when a rock called shale is squashed deep below ground. Slate naturally splits into thin sheets that make great roof tiles.

Marble

Marble forms when limestone rock is heated underground. Heating and squeezing make the rock change colour and texture. Marble can be carved easily and its surface can be polished until it shines.

The Taj Mahal

The Taj Mahal is a beautiful palace in northern India. It is made of white marble and decorated with coloured marble. Marble comes in several colours – black, pink, green and white. Some marble has swirling patterns.

The dome is made of marble blocks of different colours.

Bryce Canyon

Bryce Canyon is a national park in the western United States. It is formed of layered rocks called sandstone, limestone and mudstone. Over time, water, ice and wind have carved fantastic shapes into the rocks.

Wildlife park

Animals such as deer and foxes live in Bryce Canyon. Some use the rocks for shelter. There are also birds, such as swallows, ravens and eagles.

Hoodoos

The tall rock spires of Bryce Canyon are called hoodoos. These rocky pillars are made of soft mudstone topped with harder limestone. Ice and water wear the soft mudstone away more quickly than the harder cap of rock.

Bryce Canyon facts

- The rocks of Bryce Canyon formed on the beds of lakes and rivers. Over millions of years, the forces that build mountains lifted these rocks 2500 metres above sea level.

- Bryce Canyon has more hoodoos than almost any place on the Earth.

Water, ice and wind wear grooves in the rock.

Colourful rocks

The rocks of Bryce Canyon are pink and orange. The minerals iron and manganese give the rocks their colour. At sunrise and sunset, the rocks glow bright red.

← A bald eagle's wings can measure 2.5 metres across.

Rock arch

Thunderstorms and hailstorms can strike Bryce Canyon in summer. Snow and ice cover the ground in winter. Rain, hail, snow and ice wear away the rocks to make amazing features like this arch below.

Did you know?

Bryce Canyon became a national park in 1928. The park covers 145 square kilometres. The hoodoos of Bryce Canyon are up to 60 metres tall.

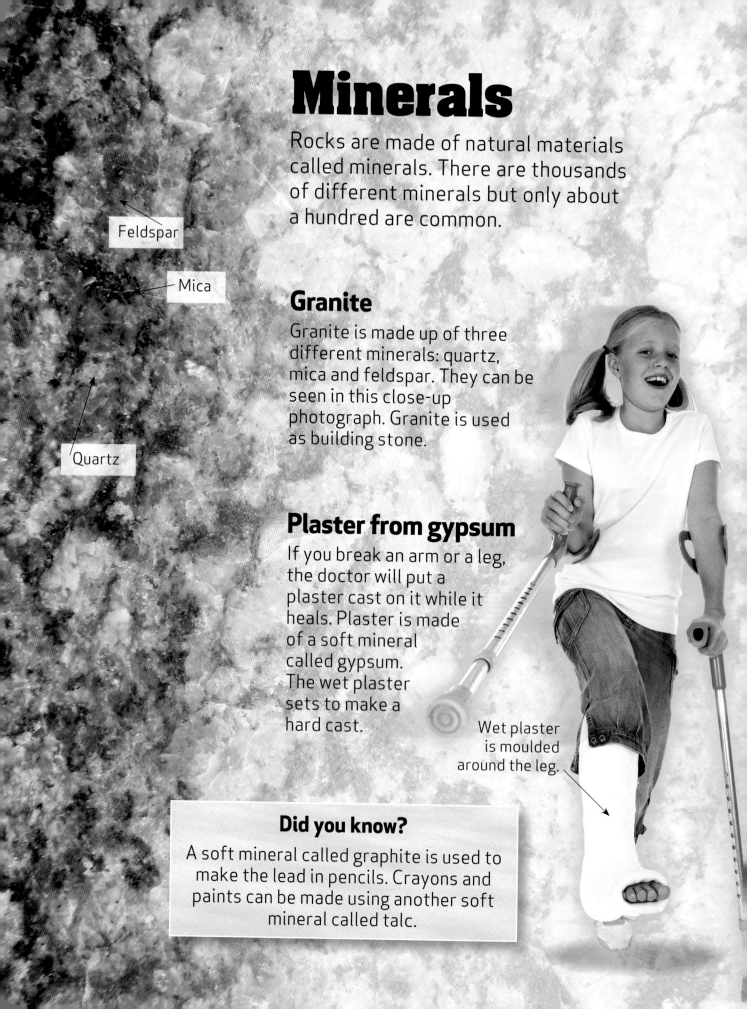

Minerals

Rocks are made of natural materials called minerals. There are thousands of different minerals but only about a hundred are common.

Feldspar

Mica

Quartz

Granite

Granite is made up of three different minerals: quartz, mica and feldspar. They can be seen in this close-up photograph. Granite is used as building stone.

Plaster from gypsum

If you break an arm or a leg, the doctor will put a plaster cast on it while it heals. Plaster is made of a soft mineral called gypsum. The wet plaster sets to make a hard cast.

Wet plaster is moulded around the leg.

Did you know?

A soft mineral called graphite is used to make the lead in pencils. Crayons and paints can be made using another soft mineral called talc.

Copper mines

Valuable minerals, such as copper, are dug from mines. Many mines run deep below ground, but copper is often found near the surface. Copper is used to make water pipes and electrical wire.

Fireworks

Fireworks, such as sparklers, can be made from a yellow mineral called sulphur. Sulphur is also used to make matches and explosives. Next time you see a firework display, remember sulphur!

Metals

Strong, shiny metals can be worked into different shapes. Metals are found in rocks called ores, often mixed with other minerals. Rare metals, such as gold, are expensive.

Lump of gold ore

Gold
wedding ring

Did you know?

The largest gold nugget ever found weighed 70 kilograms. It was found in Victoria, Australia, in 1869. The lump was nicknamed the Welcome Stranger!

Gold

Gold is usually found in rocks deep below ground. But a few lucky people have found whole lumps, called nuggets, at the surface! Specks of gold are sometimes washed out of rocks by water, and are found on river beds.

Silver

Silver is another rare metal found in an ore. Ores are usually crushed and heated to get the metal out. In the past, silver was sometimes used to make coins.

These silver coins come from Ancient Greece.

Gold rush

When someone discovers gold, thousands of people rush to the same area, hoping to get rich. This is called a gold rush. Gold in river gravel is collected by swirling the gravel around in a pan. The gold sinks to the bottom. This is called panning.

A miner panning for gold in California, United States.

Making iron

Iron is made by heating iron ore in a hot furnace, or oven. Limestone and coke (a type of coal) are also added. Hot, liquid iron runs out at the bottom of the furnace. Iron is used to make an even stronger metal called steel.

Red-hot, runny iron flows from the furnace into a container.

Gems and Jewels

Minerals called gemstones can be made into jewels. Experts cut and polish the gems until they sparkle. There are more than 50 different sorts of gemstones. They are all rare, but some are very rare.

Rough diamond

A diamond forms when a material called carbon is heated and squeezed very hard underground. Diamonds do not have much sparkle when they come out of the ground. Many sides are cut into the gem to make it sparkle.

Uncut diamond

Did you know?

Diamonds are one of the hardest minerals found on the Earth. They are used to make cutting tools as well as jewels.

This diamond has been cut and polished so it sparkles.

Crystals

Most gemstones form as even-sided crystals. Each type of crystal has a regular shape with a certain number of sides. You can see the large, purple crystals in this chunk of amethyst.

Many colours

Gemstones come in many beautiful colours. Sapphires are blue, emeralds are bright green and rubies and garnets are dark red. Opals have many colours. They are not cut with many sides but are smoothed and rounded.

Most large opals come from Australia.

Crown jewels

The crown of the British king or queen has more than 3000 jewels! One of the largest stones is a famous diamond called the Cullinan II Diamond. The largest red stone is called the Black Prince's Ruby.

Fossil Fuels

Most of the energy we use at home comes from coal, oil and gas. They are formed from fossils: the remains of prehistoric plants and animals. That's why we call them fossil fuels.

A lump of coal

Coal mining

Coal is usually found deep below ground in layers called seams. A deep hole called a shaft is dug to reach the coal. Coal is burned in power stations to produce electricity for homes and factories.

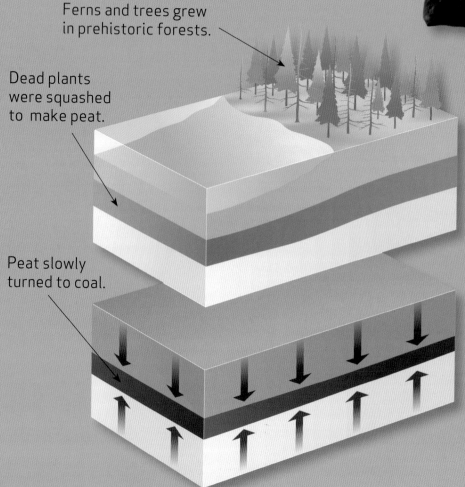

Ferns and trees grew in prehistoric forests.

Dead plants were squashed to make peat.

Peat slowly turned to coal.

How coal was made

Coal formed when prehistoric plants from swampy forests died and sank into the swamp. They were squashed as soil and rock built up on top and slowly hardened into peat, a type of soil. The peat then slowly hardened into coal.

Oil and gas

Oil and gas are the remains of tiny sea creatures that were buried and squashed on the seabed. They slowly turned to oil and gas. These fuels are mined from the seabed by drilling deep holes. Oil is made into petrol for cars. Gas is used for cooking and heating.

Cars burn fuel to power their engines.

Did you know?

When cars, factories and power stations burn fossil fuels, they give off waste gases that cause pollution. This is thought to be making the world's climate warmer. Find out more about this on pages 168–169.

All these plastic objects are made from oil.

Made from oil

Oil has many uses. Plastic and nylon are made from the leftovers when oil is purified. Paint, lipstick and candles are also made from oil.

Soil Story

You may not think of soil as valuable. But in a way, soil is even more precious than gold, oil or diamonds. Plants need soil to grow, and animals need plants for food. So most living things depend on soil.

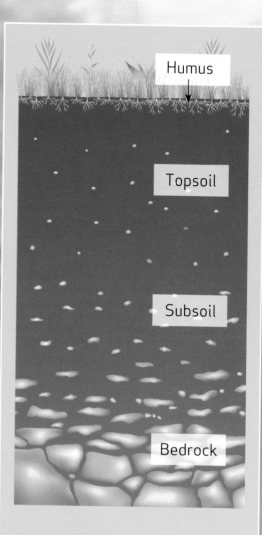

Humus

Topsoil

Subsoil

Bedrock

How soil is made

Soil is made from tiny bits of rock mixed with plant and animal remains. Soil begins to form when ice, water and wind break rocks into pieces. Plants take root in the rocky pieces. Rotting plants and animal remains make the soil richer.

Soil layers

Soil contains several layers. At the very top is a thin layer of rotting plants called humus. The rich topsoil contains plant and animal remains. The subsoil below contains broken rocks. At the bottom is solid bedrock.

Tree roots

Trees spread their roots through the soil. The roots draw water and nourishing minerals from the soil. They also anchor the tree in windy weather. Roots break up rocks to form more soil.

Different soils

There are many types of soil. Sandy and chalky soils are dry and powdery. Clay soil is sticky. Different plants like different types of soil. Gardeners need to choose the right plants for the soil in their garden.

Did you know?

It takes hundreds of years to form even a thin layer of soil. Soil is much deeper in some places than others. It may be anything from a few centimetres to several metres deep.

Life in Soil

Soil contains thousands of different living things, from tiny insects and spiders to earthworms and larger animals, such as moles and rabbits. The crops that provide our food grow in soil.

Animal burrows

Earthworms and moles burrow in the soil. Their tunnels let air and water in. This helps to make the soil more fertile. Worms and moles spend most of their lives under the ground.

Eat and be eaten

Living things in the soil depend on one another for food. Earthworms feed on rotting leaves. Moles feed on earthworms. When animals die their remains nourish the soil, which helps more plants to grow.

Moles shovel away the soil using their powerful front claws.

These oxen are pulling a plough in India.

Did you know?

Scientists say that every cubic metre of soil contains several billion living things. Most of these are so small you would need a microscope to see them.

Ploughing the soil

Farmers prepare the soil for growing crops by ploughing. This turns the soil over and helps air and water reach the lower layers. The plough can be pulled by a tractor or by animals, such as oxen or horses.

This combine harvester is pouring ripe grain into a truck.

Harvest time

Farmers harvest crops when they have grown and ripened. Some farmers cut the crop by hand. Others use a machine called a combine harvester to cut and gather the crop.

The Earth's Crust

The Earth's hard outer crust sits on top of red-hot, squishy rock. The crust is not one solid layer but is made of giant slabs of rock. The huge slabs are called plates.

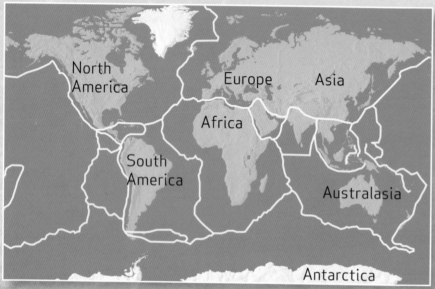

These yellow lines show the edges of the Earth's plates.

Moving plates

The Earth's plates fit together like pieces in an enormous jigsaw puzzle. Currents in the melted rock below cause the plates to drift very slowly. These movements produce earthquakes and volcanoes on the Earth's surface.

Faults

As the Earth's plates move very slowly across the surface, they bump and scrape one another. Where two plates scrape together, a long crack called a fault sometimes appears.

A fault at the point where two plates meet in Iceland.

Volcanoes

The Earth's crust is thin and weak where the plates meet. Red-hot, melted rock wells up from below, breaks through and spills out onto the surface. We call these places volcanoes (see pages 66–71).

Earthquakes

Plates moving past each other sometimes jolt violently. The jolt, which makes the ground shake, is called an earthquake (see pages 72–77). Earthquakes can do great damage.

Did you know?

The Earth's plates usually move very, very slowly. They shift about 2.5 centimetres each year. People's fingernails grow at about the same rate.

An earthquake has made this building in Japan collapse.

Volcanic Eruptions

When melted rock, called lava, spills out of a volcano, it is called an eruption. Lava rushes out in fiery rivers, then cools to form solid rock. It slowly builds up in layers to form a mountain.

Inside a volcano

Red-hot rock inside the Earth is called magma. Magma builds up below the volcano in a magma chamber. As more magma rises, the pressure builds up. Red-hot lava, ash, gas and steam burst out through the top of the volcano.

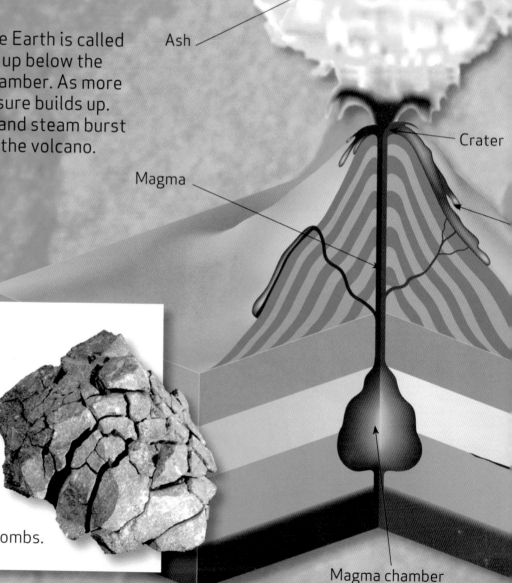

Ash

Crater

Magma

Magma chamber

Flying rocks

Some volcanoes shoot chunks of red-hot rocks high in the air. The hot rocks fly through the air and then splatter on the ground. These deadly rocks are called lava bombs.

Lava shoots out of the crater of a volcano in Hawaii.

Did you know?

In 1815, a volcano in South-East Asia called Mount Tambora shot millions of tonnes of ash into the air. The ash cloud drifted on the wind and spread all around the world. It was the most powerful eruption since records began.

Hollow crater

The opening in the top of the volcano is called the crater. As the eruption dies down, the large hole gets blocked by ash and solid lava. These shoot out with great force the next time the volcano erupts.

Lava

Glowing clouds

During some eruptions, clouds of burning ash pour out of the volcano. These heavy clouds spill down the mountain, moving much faster than lava. They burn anything in their path.

A huge cloud of ash erupts from Mount Mayon, a volcano in the Philippines.

Types of Volcano

The shape of a volcano depends on the type of lava that spills out of it. The two main types of volcanoes are tall, cone-shaped volcanoes and flatter shield volcanoes.

Underwater volcanoes

Some volcanoes erupt under the sea. The hot lava cools as soon as it hits the water. This forms rounded lumps of rock called pillow lava.

Cone-shaped volcanoes

Some volcanoes explode violently, throwing out thick, sticky lava. This type of lava flows only a short way before cooling and turning solid. Layers of lava and ash build up to form a cone-shaped mountain.

A cone-shaped volcano in the Philippines.

A shield volcano on the islands of Hawaii.

Shield volcanoes

Some volcanoes erupt runny lava. This lava flows a long way before cooling and turning solid. A low, rounded hill called a shield volcano eventually forms.

Snow covers the top of a dormant volcano in Africa.

Sleeping volcano

Not all volcanoes erupt all the time. A volcano that has not erupted for a long time but may erupt again is called a dormant volcano. 'Dormant' means 'sleeping'. A volcano that has completely stopped erupting is called an extinct volcano.

Did you know?

Volcanoes that have erupted recently, or are still erupting, are called active volcanoes. There are more than 1500 active volcanoes around the world, but only 50 to 60 actually erupt each year.

Mount St Helens

In May 1980, a volcano called Mount St Helens in the western United States suddenly erupted. The whole top of the mountain blew off in a violent explosion.

Before the eruption

Mount St Helens had not erupted for 123 years before the 1980 eruption. The mountain looked peaceful, but inside the pressure was slowly building.

Whoosh!

When Mount St Helens erupted, ash, gas and steam escaped with an enormous 'whoosh'. People living hundreds of kilometres away heard the explosion. A thick layer of ash rained down on the countryside.

Wrecked forests

Forests of tall trees covered the lower slopes of Mount St Helens before the eruption. The blast snapped the trees like matchsticks.

Eruption facts

🌏 The cloud of ash from Mount St Helens rose 20 kilometres in the sky. The ash made the sky dark and drifted on the wind to settle over a wide area. Towns up to 300 kilometres away were covered in ash.

🌏 Mount St Helens erupted violently for four days. Smaller eruptions continued for several months afterwards.

New life

After the eruption, Mount St Helens looked lifeless. Ash lay thick on the ground and choked lakes and rivers. After just a few months, plants began to sprout and animals returned to Mount St Helens.

Earthquakes

The plates that form the Earth's crust are always moving slowly. This puts the rocks below ground under great strain. An earthquake happens when the rocks suddenly jolt into a new position.

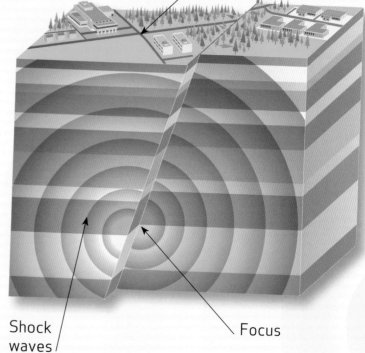

The epicentre is the point on the surface directly above the focus.

Shock waves

Focus

Shock waves

Earthquakes usually start deep underground. The point where rocks grind and shatter is called the focus. Shock waves spread out in all directions. The damage is worst on the surface directly above.

A building torn apart by the force of an earthquake.

Wrecked buildings

Powerful earthquakes make the ground shake. Buildings can be torn from their foundations. Glass shatters and steel beams bend like rubber. Houses sway and crash to the ground.

Did you know?

Thousands of earthquakes strike each year, but most are tiny. Small quakes make lightbulbs swing and ornaments rattle. The most powerful earthquakes wreck whole towns.

Cracked ground

When an earthquake strikes, the violent shaking can make the ground split open. Huge cracks can appear in roads and pavements. Some cracks are big enough to swallow cars!

This crack appeared in a road after an earthquake in California in 1989.

Broken bridge

Strong earthquakes can damage roads and bridges. In 1995, an earthquake in Japan destroyed this motorway. Wrecked roads and railways can make it difficult for outside help to reach a region hit by an earthquake.

Effects of Earthquakes

An earthquake lasts only a few seconds, but the shaking can do terrible damage. Earthquakes also start fires, cause landslides and turn solid ground to mud.

Fire!

Fires start when gas pipes and electricity lines are damaged by earthquakes. In 1989, fire swept through San Francisco, United States, after an earthquake. Water pipes were damaged by the earthquake, making it difficult for firefighters to put out the flames.

Dam burst

Powerful earthquakes can destroy dams built on rivers. A wall of water then bursts through the dam and rushes downriver. Towns and villages lower down get swept away. This dam in Taiwan was wrecked by an earthquake in 1989.

The landslide started on this hillside.

Landslide

When the ground shakes, loose soil and rock can slip away in a landslide. This landslide happened after a quake in Central America in 2001.

Did you know?

In 1970, an earthquake in the Andes Mountains made a mass of snow slide off a high peak. A tide of mud, rock and ice roared down the mountain and destroyed a town called Yungay.

Sinking ground

Violent shaking can turn clay or sandy soil to mud. Buildings sink into the mud or topple over. These blocks of flats collapsed after an earthquake hit Niigata in Japan in 1964.

Tsunamis

Earthquakes can strike under the sea as well as on land. When an earthquake shakes the seabed, it can cause enormous waves called tsunamis. These waves race across the ocean and wreck towns when they reach the coast.

2004 tsunami

In December 2004, a strong earthquake rocked the seabed off Indonesia in South-East Asia. Giant waves spread out like ripples. The waves travelled nearly 5000 kilometres to wreck towns on the shores of India and even Africa.

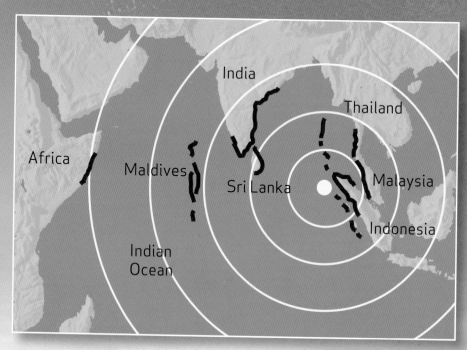

India

Thailand

Africa

Maldives

Sri Lanka

Malaysia

Indonesia

Indian Ocean

Key to map

— Areas hit by the tsunami

● Epicentre

◎ Waves spreading outwards

All the buildings in this town in Indonesia were destroyed by the 2004 tsunami.

Krakatoa

Volcanic eruptions can also cause tsunamis. In 1883, a volcano on an island called Krakatoa, in Indonesia, erupted. The explosive eruption set off tsunamis that spread far and wide. The waves swamped coastal towns, and 36,000 people died.

Towering waves

Out at sea, tsunamis form low waves that aren't very noticeable. They build up to become much taller when they reach shallow water. The huge waves are a terrifying sight when they smash onto the shore.

Did you know?

When Krakatoa exploded, the bang was heard 5000 kilometres away. The explosion destroyed most of the island, but fresh flows of lava formed a new island. The new island was named *Anak Krakatoa*, which means Child of Krakatoa.

Wrecked coast

Damage from the 2004 tsunami was worst on the coast of Indonesia. Whole towns were completely flattened by the waves. Boats were swept onto the shore and carried far inland.

MOUNTAINS AND GLACIERS

Mountains are the highest places on the Earth. This chapter explains how these rocky peaks form and describes some of the plants and animals that live there. Read on to find out about mountain dangers and about living in, and visiting, these high places. This chapter also explains what glaciers are and how they form.

Snow-covered K2
is 8611 metres tall.

Towering Mountains

Mountains are high, rocky areas that
rise above their surroundings. Many
mountains have steep, sloping sides, and
the tops of very high mountains are cold
and covered with snow.

South
America

Andes

Mountain chains

Some mountains stand alone, but many form
long lines called chains, or are found in groups
called ranges. The Andes in South America is
the longest mountain chain on land, stretching
for 7200 kilometres.

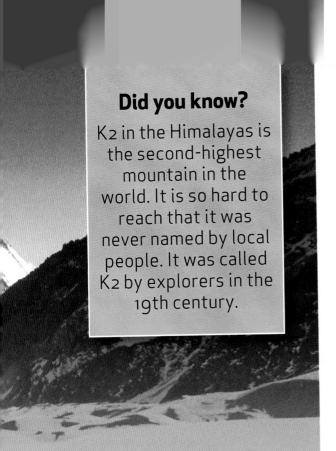

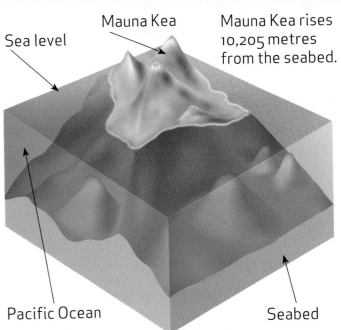

Sea level

Mauna Kea

Mauna Kea rises 10,205 metres from the seabed.

Pacific Ocean

Seabed

Rising from the ocean

Mountains are usually measured from sea level. Mauna Kea, a mountain in Hawaii, rises 4205 metres above the surface of the sea, but the rest of the peak lies underwater. Mauna Kea is taller than Mount Everest when measured from the seabed.

The Himalayas

The Himalayas in southern Asia are the world's highest mountains. This mighty range includes Mount Everest, which at 8848 metres is the Earth's highest mountain on land.

Africa's highest peak

Mount Kilimanjaro is the tallest peak in Africa. This mountain rises to 5895 metres. The top is covered with snow even though Kilimanjaro is near the Equator, where the climate is hot.

Fold Mountains

Many of the world's highest mountains are found in places where two plates of the Earth's crust push against each other. Rocks are pushed upwards, forming fold mountains.

Fold mountains in the Pyrenees in Spain

How fold mountains form

Fold mountain ranges form where two of the Earth's plates press together. The land in between the plates is pushed up and the rocks fold, forming mountain peaks. The Himalayas in Asia and the Pyrenees and the Alps in Europe are fold mountain ranges.

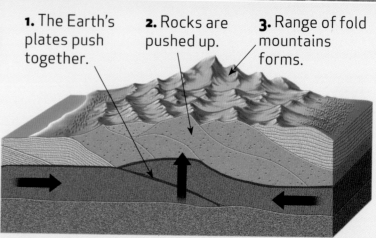

1. The Earth's plates push together.

2. Rocks are pushed up.

3. Range of fold mountains forms.

Zigzag rocks

As the layers of this rock in the UK were squashed, they folded to form these amazing zigzag patterns.

Volcanic mountains

Volcanoes are another type of mountain. These form when hot, melted rock erupts on to the Earth's surface. Layers of erupted rock build up to make tall, cone-shaped mountains (see page 68).

Cotopaxi is a volcanic mountain in Ecuador, South America.

Blocks and Domes

Two other types of mountains are steep-sided block mountains and rounded dome mountains. Mountains can take millions of years to form, but some are much older than others. Young mountains are usually much higher than old mountains.

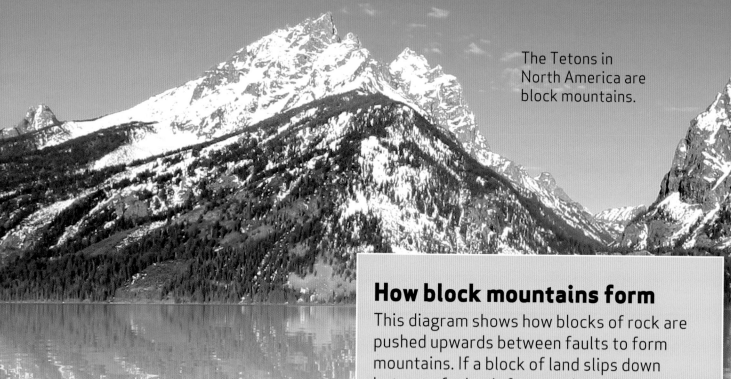

The Tetons in North America are block mountains.

Block mountains

The movement of the Earth's plates sometimes causes long cracks, called faults, to appear (see page 64). If a huge slab of rock is pushed upwards between two faults, it makes a steep-sided peak called a block mountain.

How block mountains form

This diagram shows how blocks of rock are pushed upwards between faults to form mountains. If a block of land slips down between faults, it forms a deep, flattish valley. This is called a rift valley.

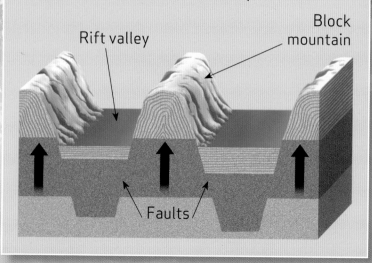

Rift valley

Block mountain

Faults

How dome mountains form

Dome mountains form where hot, melted rock pushes up but cools before it reaches the surface. The layered rocks on top are pushed up into a dome shape. Later, the rocks on top wear away to reveal the dome of volcanic rock.

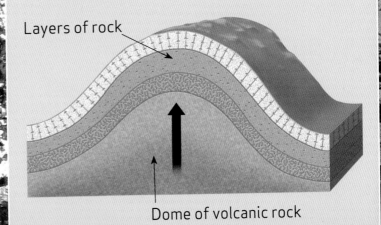

Layers of rock

Dome of volcanic rock

Did you know?

Ben Nevis, the highest peak in Britain, is 1344 metres tall and is part of the Grampian range in Scotland. The Grampians were once as high as the Himalayas, but have worn down over millions of years.

Worn smooth

Mountains are slowly worn away by the weather. Over millions of years, high, jagged mountains become lower and smoother. Ben Nevis (left) in Scotland is a very old dome mountain with a rounded top.

Mount Everest

At 8848 metres tall, Mount Everest is the world's highest mountain. This famous peak lies in the Himalayas, on the border between Nepal and Tibet in China. The mountain's local name, Chomolungma, means 'mother goddess of the world'.

Snow covers the bare, rocky slopes of Mount Everest.

Did you know?

Lhotse, the world's fourth-highest mountain, lies very close to Everest. The two mountains are linked by a snowy ridge.

Climbing Everest

The first climbers to reach the top of Everest were Edmund Hillary from New Zealand and Tenzing Norgay from Nepal in 1953. Since then many others have climbed the mountain even though it is difficult and dangerous.

Mount Everest facts

- The height of Everest was first measured by surveyors in the 1800s. They named it after Sir George Everest, a famous British surveyor.
- Italian Reinhold Messner was the first person to climb Everest alone and without using bottled oxygen to help him breathe.
- More than 4000 people have reached the top of Everest.

Sherpas

Sherpas are mountain people who live in the Everest region of Nepal. These people are used to the cold and are very fit. Some work as mountain guides and others carry loads up the steep slopes.

Sherpas balance heavy loads on their backs.

Sherpa town

Namche Bazaar is the biggest village near Everest. Sherpas live there. Not long ago the village was tiny, but now climbers and walkers stay there on their way to Everest. Namche Bazaar has become a busy town.

Cliffs and Crags

Rain, wind and ice can carve mountains into amazing shapes, including steep cliffs, uneven craggy rocks and tall, rocky pillars.

Monument Valley

This valley in the western United States has many craggy, flat-topped rocks. This rock is one of a pair called the Mittens. Can you guess why?

Wind and rain have worn away the rock to leave a tall pillar.

Devil's marbles

These amazing rocks are found in the Tanami Desert in Australia. It is very hot there in the day and freezing at night. The heat and the cold make the rocks flake. This has formed rounded shapes that look like giant marbles.

Uluru

This mass of sandstone rock in central Australia is called Uluru. The 348-metre-tall rock is all that is left of a mountain range that once covered the area.

Did you know?

Uluru is also called Ayers Rock. It is a holy place for the Aboriginals, the native people of Australia.

Dartmoor tors

Rocky hills called tors are made of a hard fiery rock called granite. Frost and rain crack the rocks and help form the craggy shapes. Many tors are found on Dartmoor in southern England.

Mountain Habitats

Mountains have extreme weather conditions with long, icy winters. The weather is often windy, rainy or snowy. Mountain plants and animals have to be tough to cope.

Brrrrr!

Mountain air is thinner (contains less gas) than air in the lowlands. Thin air can hold less of the Sun's heat, so the higher up you climb the colder it gets.

People who live on or visit the mountains have to wear warm clothes to keep out the cold.

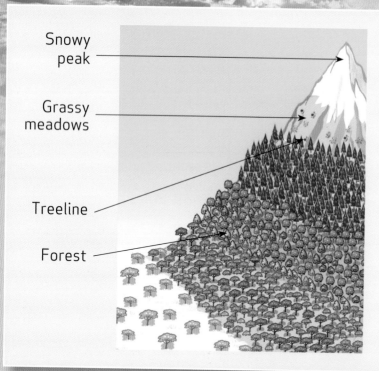

Snowy peak

Grassy meadows

Treeline

Forest

Mountain plants

Different plants grow at different heights on mountains. Trees only grow on lower slopes. At the top, no plants can grow, and snow covers the bare rock. On the middle slopes, there are grassy meadows filled with flowers.

Trees do not grow on mountains above a point called the treeline.

Mountain animals

Animals that live high on mountains have thick hair to keep them warm. Birds have extra-warm feathers. This llama lives in the Andes. Llamas have large lungs that help them breathe the thin mountain air.

Did you know?

Animals called marmots live on high mountains in many parts of the world. They stay there all year, spending the winter sleeping in their burrows. This is called hibernation.

Moving up and down

These goat-like animals, called chamois, live in the Alps. They move up the mountain to eat grass in summer. In autumn, they move down to the valley to shelter there throughout the cold winter.

Rubbery hooves grip the slippery rocks.

Icy Glaciers

Glaciers are found in high mountains. They are rivers of ice that move very slowly downhill, scraping off pieces of rock as they flow.

How do glaciers form?

On high mountains, snow does not melt but builds up into a thick layer. The snow underneath is squashed down and turns to ice. The ice gets so heavy and slippery that it starts to slide downhill.

At the end

At the lowest end of the glacier, the ice begins to melt because the air there is a bit warmer. Any pieces of rock carried along in the ice are dumped at the end of the glacier.

Deep cracks form where the ice splits.

Did you know?

The world's longest glacier is the Lambert Glacier in Antarctica. It flows for 400 kilometres from the Antarctic Mountains towards the sea.

Oetzi, the ice man

In 1991, two climbers found the remains of a prehistoric man in a glacier in the Alps. The man had died while on a mountain journey more than 5000 years ago. His body had been preserved by the ice. He was named Oetzi after the valley where he was found.

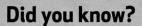

This is what Oetzi may have looked like.

Joining together

Pieces of rock are carried along the sides of glaciers, forming dark stripes called moraines. When smaller glaciers join together, the stripes meet in the middle, as can be seen in this Swiss glacier (right).

The Aletsch glacier in Switzerland is the longest in the Alps.

Worn by Glaciers

Glaciers used to cover much more of the Earth than they do today (see pages 96–97). When these glaciers melted, they left scenery shaped by ice, including U-shaped valleys and steep-sided fjords.

Did you know?

Most glaciers flow very slowly, moving one to two metres a day. Some glaciers can flow much faster – up to 40 metres a day in summer months.

Sheer sides

This tall, pointed peak was carved by glaciers flowing down all sides of the mountain. It is called the Matterhorn and is found in the Alps on the border between Switzerland and Italy.

U-shaped valleys

As a glacier flows downhill, it acts like a giant bulldozer. The ice gouges out a deep valley with a flat bottom. Rocks and boulders carried along beneath the glacier scrape away more soil and rock.

A glacier carved this deep, U-shaped valley in Wales.

Mountain tarns

Small, round lakes called tarns were carved by glaciers. The ice gouged out bowl-shaped hollows high up on mountains. When the ice melted, the hollows filled with water.

A cruise ship visits a steep-sided fjord in Norway.

Fjords

Fjords are steep-sided valleys on the coast. They were carved by glaciers thousands of years ago. Later the ice melted, and the sea rose to flood the valleys, creating fjords.

Ice Caps

In very cold places, the snow never melts. Packed-down snow builds up to form a thick layer of ice called an ice cap. In the past, ice covered much more of the Earth's surface than it does today.

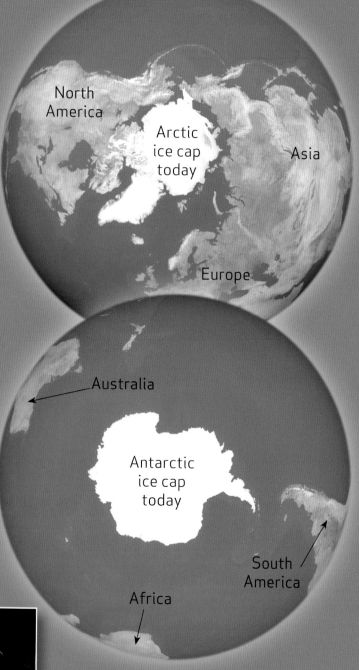

North America

Arctic ice cap today

Asia

Europe

Australia

Antarctic ice cap today

South America

Africa

Polar ice

Thick ice covers the land at the Arctic and Antarctic (see page 37). In winter, the icy area gets bigger as the sea freezes over. In summer, the sea ice melts, and the icy area shrinks again.

Ice samples, or cores, contain ice from lower layers.

Old ice

The Antarctic ice cap is up to four kilometres deep. The ice at the bottom is made of snow that fell hundreds of years ago. Scientists study the old ice to find out what conditions were like all those years ago.

Ice Ages

During long, cold periods called Ice Ages, ice covered much of Europe and North America. This map shows the area covered by ice in the last Ice Age, which ended about 10,000 years ago.

Arctic ice cap 18,000 years ago

Compare this with the map opposite, showing the Arctic ice cap today.

Did you know?

Ice covers about a tenth of the Earth's surface today. During the last Ice Age, it covered about a quarter of the planet.

Woolly mammoth

Huge, hairy elephants called mammoths lived in Asia, Europe and North America during the last Ice Age. Bodies of mammoths have been found in the ice in northern Russia. When the Ice Age ended, mammoths died out.

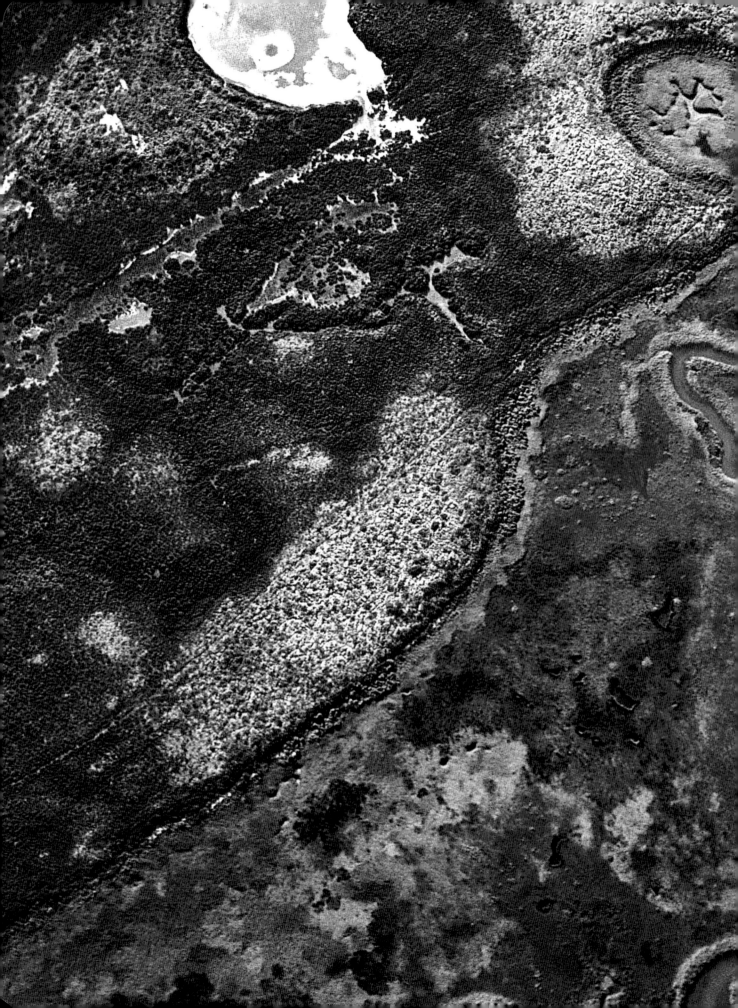

RIVERS, LAKES AND CAVES

Rivers are channels of fresh water that flow across the land. Smaller rivers called streams join bigger rivers to make mighty rivers that flow to the sea. Rivers shape the landscape, filling lakes and carving deep caves and canyons. Rivers even flow under the ground. People use rivers and lakes for transport and fun, but these watery places can also be dangerous. Find out more about rivers, lakes and caves in this chapter.

A River's Journey

A river's course is the long journey that it takes from where it begins, high in hills or mountains, to where it ends – in the sea or a lake.

The source

The place where a river starts is called the source. The water comes from rain or melted snow. It may bubble up out of the ground at a spring or trickle out of a lake or glacier.

A stream trickles down a mountain.

Course of a river

In its upper course, a river rushes down from a hill or mountain, carving deep gorges and valleys. In its middle and lower courses, a river makes wider valleys and creates flat areas called floodplains.

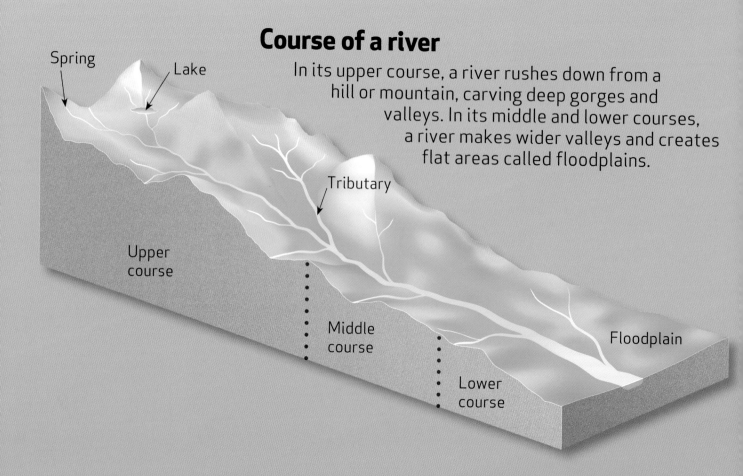

Spring

Lake

Tributary

Upper course

Middle course

Lower course

Floodplain

Wearing and shaping

As rivers flow downhill, they carry loose stones and rocks along with them. The stones bounce along the bottom of the river and scrape more soil and rocks away.

A bear walks across the rocks and stones left by a mountain river.

Did you know?

The River Nile is the world's longest river. It begins in the mountains of East Africa and flows north for 6853 kilometres. The Nile empties into the Mediterranean Sea.

Joining the river

Trickles of water join to make streams. Streams join to make rivers. Lower down, small rivers called tributaries join the main river. The water gets wider and deeper.

Young Rivers

At its upper course, a river is known as a young river as it flows downhill. The rushing water loosens rocks and soil, carving deep canyons and gorges.

Deepest gorge

A gorge is a steep-sided canyon. The Kali Gandaki Gorge in the Himalayas is 5.5 kilometres deep – the deepest gorge in the world. The river has cut a deep valley between two mountains.

View of the Kali Gandaki Gorge

The Grand Canyon

Canyons form where water cuts through hard rock. The Grand Canyon is a famous canyon in the United States. The Colorado River has worn a very deep valley as it has cut down through the rock.

The deep valley of the Grand Canyon.

Leaping salmon

Salmon swim up young mountain rivers to lay their eggs. They have to swim very hard against the flow of water. When they reach fast-moving water, they leap out of the water to move upstream.

These salmon are leaping up a waterfall.

Did you know?

The Grand Canyon is up to 1.6 kilometres deep and 30 kilometres wide in places.

Foaming rapids

Rapids form where young rivers plunge over stones and boulders. The white, foaming water rushes along very quickly. It is fun to ride the rapids in a rubber boat.

Waterfalls

Where a river plunges over a steep cliff, it forms a waterfall. Beautiful falls with white, foaming water can be seen on rivers in many parts of the world.

This boat takes tourists to see the waterfall up close.

Niagara Falls

Niagara Falls is a famous waterfall in North America. It lies on the border between the United States and Canada. The falls curve around like a giant horseshoe and are 51 metres high.

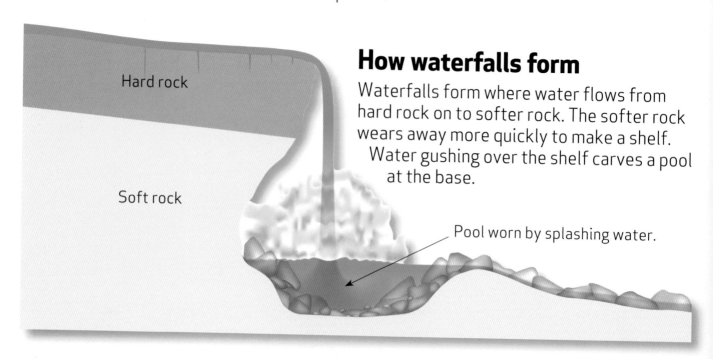

Hard rock

Soft rock

Pool worn by splashing water.

How waterfalls form

Waterfalls form where water flows from hard rock on to softer rock. The softer rock wears away more quickly to make a shelf. Water gushing over the shelf carves a pool at the base.

Angel Falls

Angel Falls in Venezuela, South America, is the world's highest waterfall. It is 979 metres tall and is located where the River Churún plunges over a steep cliff.

Did you know?

Angel Falls is named after American pilot Jimmy Angel, who spotted the waterfall from his plane in 1933.

Iguazu swifts

Iguazu Falls is a very beautiful waterfall in South America. It is 2.7 kilometres wide and drops nearly 80 metres. Small birds called swifts nest on the rockface behind the falls. The birds fly through the water to get to their nests.

In the Valley

In the middle and lower parts of its journey, the river leaves the hills behind and flows through a wide, flattish valley.

Fertile soil

A river carries mud and gravel. After heavy rain, the river may flood and spill muddy water onto the surrounding land: the floodplain. Crops grow well in the fertile soil of the floodplain.

River life

Different plants and animals live in and by the river at each stage of its journey. Herons, such as this one, hunt fish and frogs along the banks of gently flowing rivers.

A wide river and its floodplain in Colorado, United States

River loops are called meanders.

Twisting and turning

Rivers twist and turn as they flow through wide valleys. Water flows fastest on the outside of bends, cutting the bank away. Mud is dropped on the inside, where the flow is weaker. In time, gentle curves become deep loops.

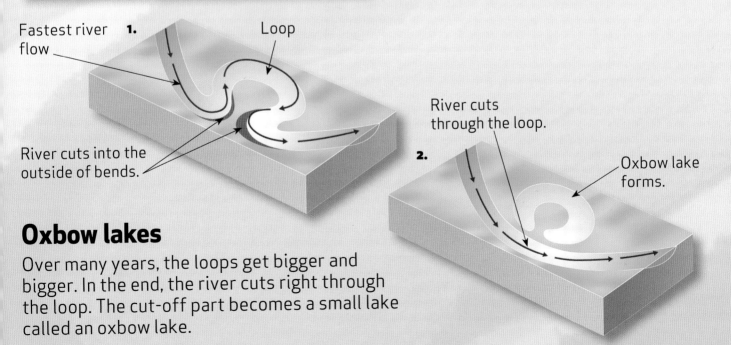

Fastest river flow

1.

Loop

River cuts into the outside of bends.

River cuts through the loop.

2.

Oxbow lake forms.

Oxbow lakes

Over many years, the loops get bigger and bigger. In the end, the river cuts right through the loop. The cut-off part becomes a small lake called an oxbow lake.

RUSSIA

KAZAKHSTAN

Caspian Sea

AZERBAIJAN

TURKMENISTAN

IRAN

Lakes

Lakes are hollows in the ground filled with water from rivers or melted ice. Some hollows were carved by glaciers. Others formed because of movements in the Earth's crust.

Largest lake

The Caspian Sea, left, is the world's largest lake. It covers 371,000 square kilometres in western Asia. Because the lake contains salty water, it is really an inland sea.

Deepest lake

Lake Baikal in Russia is the world's deepest lake. It is more than 1600 metres deep in places. This lake is home to the only type of seal that lives in fresh water: the Baikal seal.

Highest lake

Lake Titicaca in Peru is the highest lake in the world that boats sail on. It lies 3800 metres up in the Andes Mountains. Local people travel in boats such as this, made of bundles of reeds.

Did you know?

The world's largest lake containing fresh water is Lake Superior in North America. It covers 82,000 square kilometres.

Crater lakes

Some lakes form when water fills the crater of a volcano. Crater Lake (below) in Oregon is 592 metres deep. It is the deepest lake in the United States.

Reaching the Sea

The place where a river meets the sea is called its mouth. The river's flow slows as it reaches the sea, and it drops its load of sand or mud to form flat areas called estuaries or deltas.

Pink flamingos feeding in an estuary

River estuary

The estuary is the lower part of a river, where fresh water mixes with salty seawater. Worms and snails burrow in the muddy banks, providing plenty of food for birds.

Deltas

A delta forms when mud or sand builds up at a river's mouth. The delta may be triangular or shaped like a bird's foot. The river divides into many smaller channels as it flows through the delta.

The Mississippi River delta, United States, is shaped like a bird's foot.

Nile Delta

The River Nile has a huge, fan-shaped delta. Mud dumped by the river has made a triangle of fertile land. Green fields are surrounded by desert, which looks brown.

Mediterranean Sea

Nile Delta

Red Sea

EGYPT

River Nile

Did you know?

The world's largest delta is the Ganges Delta in Asia. It covers around 100,000 square kilometres and has 400 kilometres of coastline.

Nile crocodile

In the past, the Nile Delta was home to the Nile crocodile. Now farms cover the delta, and these fierce beasts are rarely seen there. They are still found in rivers, estuaries and deltas in other parts of Africa.

The Mighty Amazon

The River Amazon in South America is not as long as the Nile, but it contains far more water. The river begins high in the Andes Mountains and flows through the Amazon rainforest on its way to the sea.

Amazon facts

🌍 The Amazon flows for 6437 kilometres. The river and its tributaries cover more than seven million square kilometres – more than a third of South America.

🌍 The Amazon empties 200,000 cubic metres of water into the ocean every second. That's enough to fill 80 Olympic-sized swimming pools.

River basin

Water from an area ten times the size of France flows into the Amazon. The total area through which a river and its tributaries flow is called the river's basin.

Amazon Delta

The Amazon measures about 240 kilometres across as it reaches the ocean. The river is so wide that it looks like the sea. This picture shows water weaving between islands in the Amazon Delta.

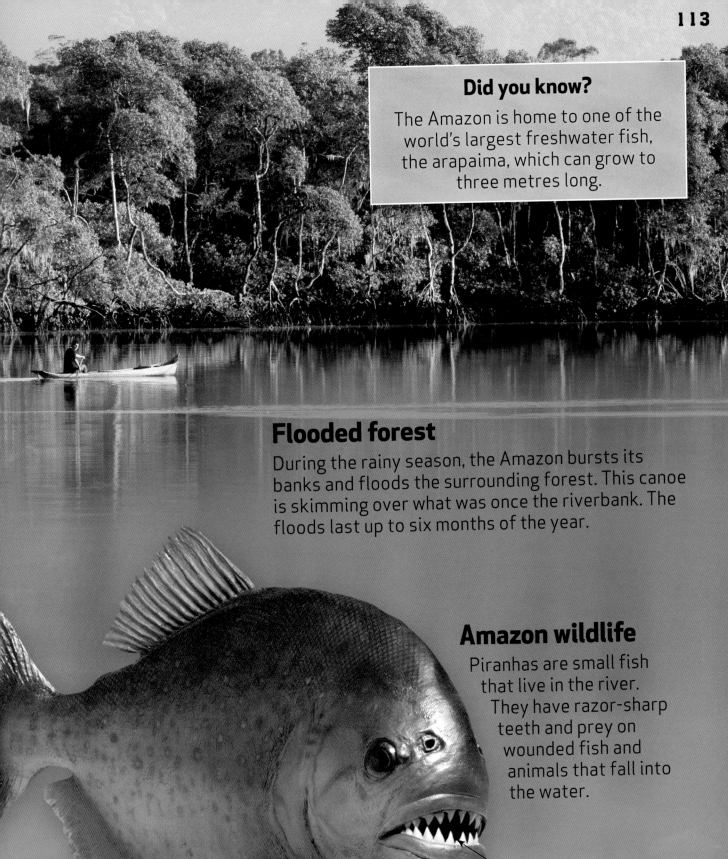

Did you know?

The Amazon is home to one of the world's largest freshwater fish, the arapaima, which can grow to three metres long.

Flooded forest

During the rainy season, the Amazon bursts its banks and floods the surrounding forest. This canoe is skimming over what was once the riverbank. The floods last up to six months of the year.

Amazon wildlife

Piranhas are small fish that live in the river. They have razor-sharp teeth and prey on wounded fish and animals that fall into the water.

If a piranha loses a tooth, a new one grows.

Underground Rivers

Water flows under the ground as well as over it. Water running under the ground can wear away some types of rock to make deep, dark caves.

Gaping Gill, a pothole in England, is 111 metres deep.

Disappearing water

Water eats into a type of soft rock called limestone. Over time, it makes deep holes called sinkholes (or potholes) and runs under the ground. The water wears away the rock beneath the surface, forming hollow caves.

Limestone caves

Water can form huge caves in limestone rock, linked by underground tunnels. Water falling through sinkholes can carve out deep pools. Rock formations called stalactites and stalagmites (see page 116) are often seen in caves.

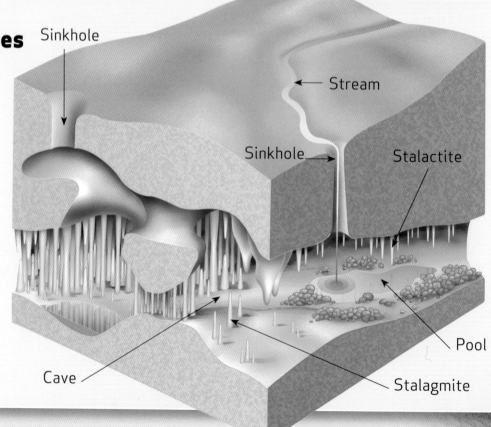

Sinkhole

Stream

Sinkhole

Stalactite

Pool

Cave

Stalagmite

Wells

If you dig down deep enough almost anywhere on the Earth, you will reach water. People dig holes called wells and drop buckets down them to bring water to the surface.

Desert oasis

Water cannot soak through all types of rock. When it reaches a layer of rock it cannot pass through, water runs sideways. Sometimes the water reaches the surface again and bubbles out in a spring. In a desert, such a place is called an oasis.

A boy draws water from a well in Afghanistan, Asia.

An oasis in Libya, Africa

Stalactites hang down from the ceiling.

Amazing Caves

In some places on the Earth, a secret world lies underground, where caves and tunnels run for kilometres. Exploring this hidden world is called potholing.

Stalagmites and stalactites

Stalagmites and stalactites are stony pillars found in caves. They are made by dripping water. The water contains a mineral called calcite, which builds up to make the pillars.

Stalagmites rise from the floor.

Potholers

Potholers wear waterproof clothes and a helmet with a light on when they explore these dark, wet places. This potholer is looking at a stalactite.

Bat caves

Many bats like dark places. They sleep in caves by day and hunt for food at night. Bats hang upside down from cave walls using their sharp claws.

Cave paintings

In prehistoric times, some people lived in caves. They painted pictures of the animals they hunted on cave walls. This painting in a French cave is more than 15,000 years old.

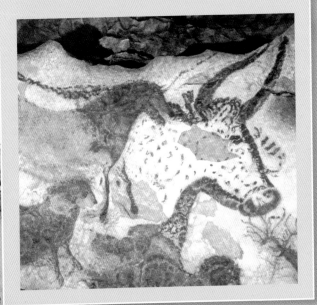

Did you know?

The largest group of linked caves and tunnels is the Mammoth Cave System in Kentucky, United States. The caves run for 640 kilometres.

Using Rivers

Rivers provide water for drinking, washing and cleaning. People also use rivers to water crops, run factories and make electricity. It's no wonder people live beside rivers all over the world.

Cities on rivers

Most of the world's oldest towns and villages were built beside rivers. Some of these are now capital cities, such as London and Paris. The Houses of Parliament (below) in London are next to the River Thames.

Water for farming

River water is vital for farming. These green fields beside the River Nile are watered by the river. Without the Nile, this place would be a desert.

Water for energy

Hydroelectric stations use energy from fast-flowing water to make electricity. A dam is often built to control the flow of water. This is Glen Canyon Dam in Arizona, United States.

Factories by rivers

Factories of all kinds use river water to power machinery, and also for cleaning. Paper mills, like this one, use huge amounts of water every day.

Did you know?

Glen Canyon Dam is 216 metres high. A huge lake called Lake Powell has built up behind the dam. The lake supplies water to nearby cities.

River Safety

Rivers can be dangerous places. Floods can strike after heavy rain, damaging roads and houses. Dirty river water can also harm people and animals.

These people are stacking sandbags to try to keep the Mississippi floodwater away from their homes.

Mississippi floods

In 1993, the Mississippi River in the United States burst its banks. Floodwater covered more than 70,000 square kilometres. About 70,000 people had to leave their homes.

Floods in China

When the Yangtze River in China flooded in 1998, this family escaped by boat. Sadly, more than 3000 people died and about 14 million were made homeless.

Did you know?

In China, the Yellow River is called 'China's sorrow' because it has caused such bad flooding. In 1938, up to 400,000 people died when the river burst its banks.

Water pollution

River water can be polluted (made dirty) by sewage or waste from farms and factories. This can harm people. Many countries now have strict rules to stop river pollution.

This pipe is emptying dirty water into a river.

Preventing floods

During very high tides (see pages 126–127), seawater could flood London. The Thames Barrier was built to protect the city. It has huge gates that can be shut to prevent seawater flowing into the river.

SEAS AND OCEANS

The oceans are a vast world that we are
still exploring and finding out about. This
chapter will explain how waves, tides and
currents affect the ocean and shape the
land. It will tell you how coasts, islands
and coral reefs form. You can also find
out about creatures that live at different
depths in the oceans, including the deep
sea: a mysterious world that we know
very little about.

Watery World

Less than a third of the Earth's surface is land. Salty water covers the rest. This huge expanse of water is divided into areas called oceans and seas.

Salty oceans

Seawater is salty because it contains minerals carried out to sea by rivers. The main minerals are sodium and chloride. These two minerals make salt.

Did you know?

The Pacific Ocean is the world's biggest ocean. It covers 166 million square kilometres and holds more than half of all the water in the oceans.

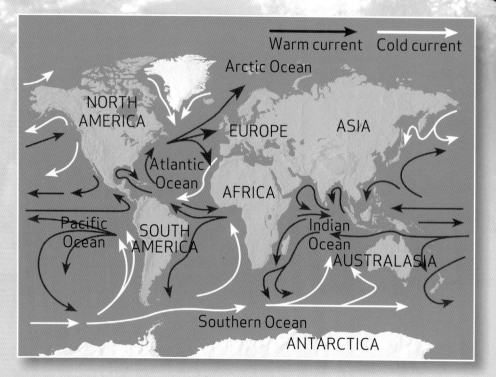

Warm current   Cold current
Arctic Ocean
NORTH AMERICA
EUROPE   ASIA
Atlantic Ocean
AFRICA
Pacific Ocean
SOUTH AMERICA
Indian Ocean
AUSTRALASIA
Southern Ocean
ANTARCTICA

Oceans and seas

The five oceans are called the Atlantic, Pacific, Indian, Arctic and Southern Oceans. They are linked by smaller areas of water called seas. Warm and cold currents flow like mighty rivers through the oceans.

Super-salty water

The Dead Sea in Asia is nine times saltier than other seas and oceans. The salt makes the water thicker, so it is easier to float. But all that salt means that nothing but bacteria lives in the Dead Sea: that's how it got its name.

Warm waters

A warm current called the Gulf Stream warms the coasts of Britain and Ireland. The current starts near Mexico and flows across the Atlantic Ocean.

Palm trees grow in the mild climate on western Irish coasts.

Waves and Tides

The water in seas and oceans is always on the move. Waves sweep across the ocean surface. The sea rises and falls on coasts as tides come and go.

How do waves form?

Winds blowing across the ocean make ripples on the surface. The ripples grow into waves, and travel across the ocean surface until they reach the shore.

Circling water

The water in a wave moves in a circle. Far out to sea, the water circles freely. Close to shore, the seabed stops water flowing in circles. This makes the waves rise up into crests.

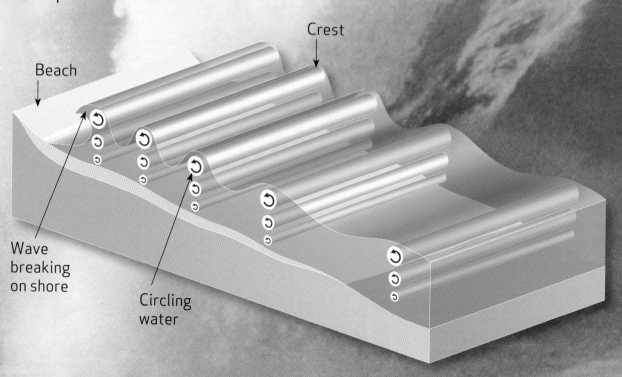

Crest

Beach

Wave breaking on shore

Circling water

Changing tides

Tides mainly happen because the Moon's gravity (see pages 18–19) pulls on the oceans. As the Moon circles the Earth, it pulls the sea towards it. A mound of water forms below the Moon. This mound is a high tide.

A surfer rides a huge wave.

High and low tides

These pictures show the same harbour in Cornwall, England, at high and low tides. At high tide, water fills the harbour. At low tide, the harbour is empty, and the boats are stranded on the sand.

High tide

Low tide

Did you know?

The Bay of Fundy in Canada has very high and very low tides. The water level changes by up to 16 metres.

Rocky Coasts

High cliffs tower above the sea on some coastlines. Other shores have wide, sandy bays, headlands or amazing rock arches. All of these landscapes are formed by the pounding waves.

Steep cliffs

Waves crash onto the shore every minute of every day. Water, grit and pebbles smash against rocky coasts, chipping bits away. Steep cliffs form where hills meet the ocean.

Headlands and bays

As waves beat against the shore, soft rocks wear away more quickly than hard rocks. The sea cuts deep, curving bays into soft rocks. Hard rocks stand up to the waves, forming headlands that stick far out to sea.

Headland

Bay

Rock arch

Rock arches form where waves eat into a headland from both sides. This makes two caves, which eventually wear right through to make an arch. This arch is in the Galapagos Islands in South America.

Arch is worn by the waves.

Direction of waves

Arch collapses to leave a stack.

Did you know?

Waves pound into cliffs and slowly wear them away. On some coasts, the land is worn away by more than a metre each year.

How stacks form

Waves continue to crash against a rock arch. Eventually, the top of the arch crumbles, leaving a pillar of rock standing in the ocean. The pillar is called a stack.

On the Beach

Beaches can be sandy or pebbly. Most people prefer a sandy beach to any other kind of beach – and some animals do too!

How do beaches form?

Rivers carry sand and rocks out to sea. Waves also chip pieces off cliffs. Beaches form where waves dump the sand and rocks in sheltered bays.

A sandy beach has formed in this bay in Cornwall, UK.

Sandy or pebbly

Sand is made of tiny bits of rock or shell. Rivers and waves have smashed the rocks and shells into tiny pieces. Pebbles on beaches are small rocks that have been worn smooth by the water.

Beach wildlife

All sorts of animals live on beaches. Crabs, worms and cockles burrow into the sand. Gulls search for fish by the water's edge. Shellfish, such as limpets, cling to the rocks.

Crabs have large claws, which they use to grab food.

Did you know?

Praia do Cassino in Brazil is one of the world's longest sandy beaches. It stretches for around 240 kilometres!

Shifting sideways

Where waves strike the shore at an angle, they shift sand and pebbles sideways. This material can pile up out to sea to make a strip of land called a spit. Groynes are fences built across a beach to stop the sand moving along the beach.

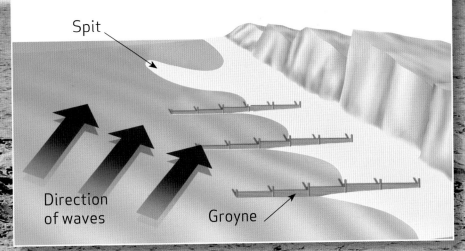

Spit

Direction of waves

Groyne

Islands

Islands are areas of land completely surrounded by water. Some islands, such as Britain, are big, but many islands are small. There are islands in rivers and lakes, as well as in the sea.

Near the mainland

Some islands lie close to large land masses called continents. Britain was once joined to mainland Europe but became an island when the sea level rose thousands of years ago.

Ireland   Britain

Europe

Volcanic islands

Islands that lie far out to sea are often the tips of underwater volcanoes. The volcano erupts on the seabed and lava builds up to make a mountain. The mountain eventually breaks the water's surface, forming an island.

A volcanic island in Alaska, United States

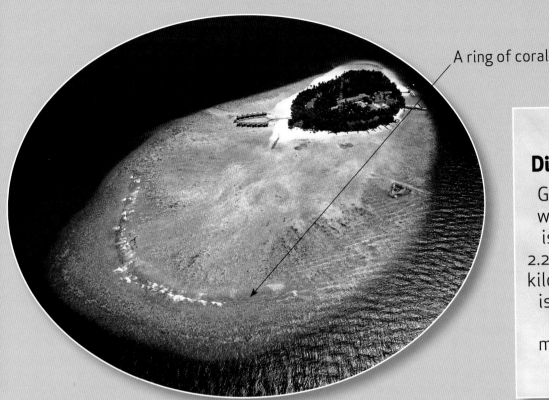

A ring of coral

Did you know?

Greenland, the world's largest island, covers 2.2 million square kilometres. Small islands may be just a few metres across.

Coral islands

This island is made of a hard material called coral (see pages 134–135). Sometimes a ring of coral forms around a small volcanic island. The island may later sink as a result of the movement of the Earth's crust, leaving just the coral.

Island life

Many remote islands are home to animals found nowhere else. The Galapagos giant tortoise lives on a group of islands called the Galapagos Islands in South America.

Great Barrier Reef

Coral reefs form in warm, shallow seas. They aren't made of rock, but are built by small creatures called coral polyps. The Great Barrier Reef, off Australia, is the world's largest coral reef.

Coral homes

Coral reefs are hard ridges just below the surface of the sea. They are home to many ocean creatures, including brightly coloured fish, shrimps and starfish. Turtles and sharks swim nearby.

Barrier Reef facts

🌏 The Great Barrier Reef is made up of 3000 smaller reefs and islands. The reef stretches for 2000 kilometres, and is so large that it can be seen from space.

🌏 More than 1500 different types of fish live on the Great Barrier Reef.

Reef builders

A coral polyp has a chalky shell and a soft body with arm-like tentacles. When a polyp dies, its shell remains. Millions of layers of shell build up on top of one another to form a coral reef.

Coral tentacles

Reef stingers

Sea anemones live on the reef. The stings of these animals kill most fish, but clownfish are safe because their bodies are protected by a special slime.

Did you know?

Coral only grows a few centimetres a year. It takes millions of years for a large reef to form.

Scary sharks

Sharks hunt in the clear waters by the reef. These big fish have a very good sense of smell. When they smell the blood of a wounded creature, they swim up for the kill.

The pointed fin sticks out of the water when a shark swims near the surface.

Jellyfish

Sunlit zone:
0–200 metres

Mackerel

Mid-depths:
200–2000
metres

Sperm
whale

Giant squid

Deep sea:
2000–4000
metres

Gulper eel

Anglerfish

Depths below
4000 metres
are called
the abyss.

Open Ocean

In the open ocean, water stretches out on all sides and for several kilometres downwards. The water can be divided into layers, with different creatures living at different depths.

Ocean layers

The upper waters are lit by the sunlight. Jellyfish and mackerel swim there. Sperm whales and giant squid swim in the dim mid-waters. Gulper eels and anglerfish live in the inky-black depths.

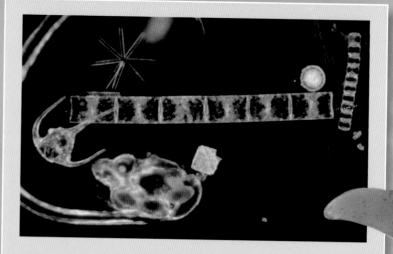

Plankton

Tiny plants and animals called plankton float in the ocean water. Many of them are so small you can only see them using a microscope. Plankton provide food for many larger creatures, including whales.

At the surface

Large, powerful fish called marlin chase after shoals of mackerel near the surface. They snap up the small fish with their long, pointed snouts.

Diving to the depths

Sperm whales come to the surface to breathe. Then they dive to depths of 1000 metres to hunt giant squid. Many sperm whales are scarred by battles with squid.

Marlin can swim at speeds of up to 80 kilometres an hour.

Did you know?

The ocean's deepest point is the Mariana Trench in the western Pacific. It lies up to 10,994 metres below the surface. In 1960, two scientists went to the bottom in a submarine.

On the Seabed

Many creatures live on the seabed. Starfish and flatfish live in fairly shallow water. Other creatures lurk on the beds of deep oceans, where there are mountains, cliffs and volcanoes similar to those on land.

Flatfish

Flatfish rest on the seabed. The speckled colours of this plaice blend in with the sand. The fish changes colour when it moves onto rock or weeds, allowing it to hide from its enemies.

Ocean floor

Long mountain chains run down the centre of the oceans. The flat plains on either side may be dotted with volcanoes or cut by deep trenches. The seabed slopes upwards to broad, flat shelves that edge the land.

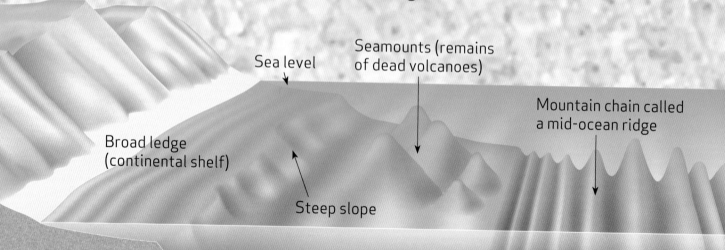

Sea level

Seamounts (remains of dead volcanoes)

Mountain chain called a mid-ocean ridge

Broad ledge (continental shelf)

Steep slope

Plain

Starfish

Starfish creep along the seabed. Most starfish have five arms, but some have up to 50. A starfish can regrow an arm if it gets bitten off by an enemy.

Plain

Mapping the seabed

Scientists map the seabed using a technique called sonar. They aim sound waves at the bottom and listen to the echoes that bounce back. The time taken by the echoes tells them how deep it is.

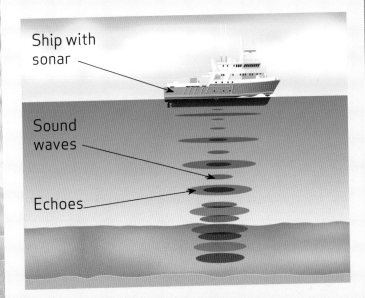

Ship with sonar

Sound waves

Echoes

The Deep Sea

The deep sea is the last unexplored place on the Earth because it is so difficult to get to. Only a few submarines can descend that deep.

Black smokers

In 1977, scientists exploring a deep-sea ridge made an amazing discovery. They found strange chimneys spouting clouds of black, boiling-hot water. These undersea volcanoes are called black smokers.

Deep-sea submarine

This special submarine can explore the bottom of the ocean. It is called *Alvin* and carries three people. *Alvin* has two arms that can collect samples.

Viperfish

Anglerfish

Brittle star

Fish of the deep

Deep-sea fish hunt in the cold, black water. Many have huge mouths and stretchy stomachs so they can swallow any prey they find. Some can swallow prey twice their own size!

Life at black smokers

Strange creatures live around the black smokers. There are blind crabs, eyeless shrimps and long, slim tube worms. The hot water, rich in minerals, helps these creatures to stay alive.

Did you know?

Deep-sea fish are built to stand the enormous pressure caused by the weight of all the water pressing down from above. Deep-sea fish can die if they get too close to the surface!

A crab near a black smoker

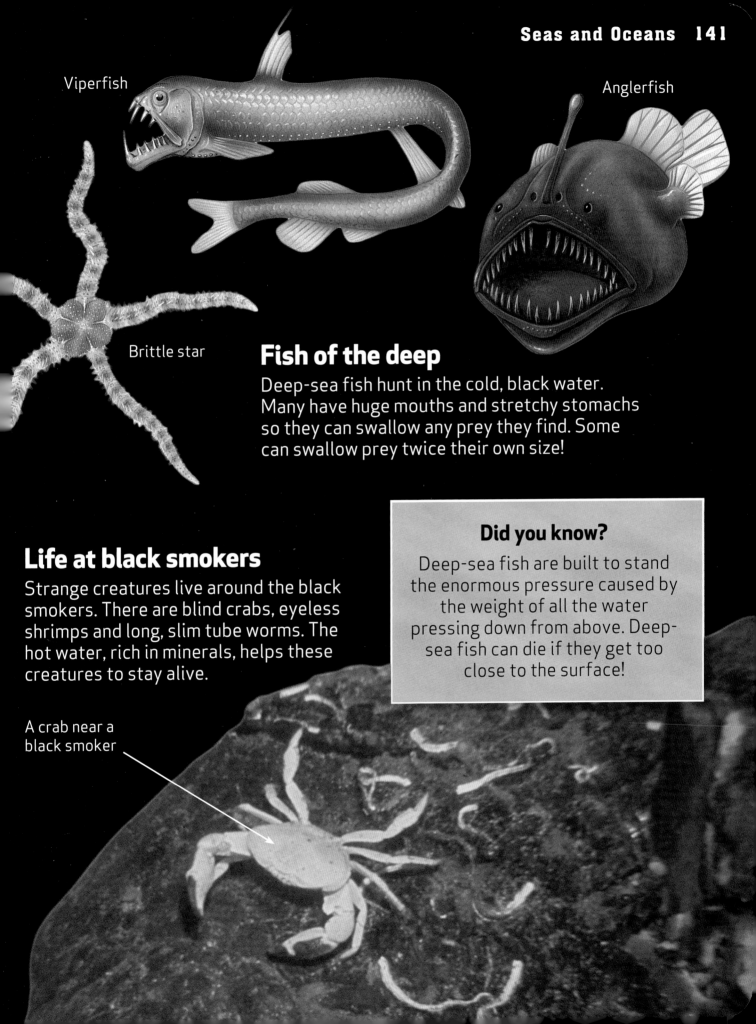

Icy Seas

The seas in the polar regions are covered with ice for much of the year. There are towering icebergs and huge, flat-topped ice shelves. When the sea freezes over, a different type of ice – pack ice – forms.

Ice shelf

Huge ice shelves edge the land in the polar regions. They form where glaciers meet the ocean, and the ice breaks off and floats out to sea.

A thick coat of feathers keeps out the cold.

Penguins

Penguins live on the coasts of Antarctica. They walk with a waddle on land, but are fast swimmers. They dive into the icy water to hunt fish. Penguins cannot fly, but they flap their wings to swim under water.

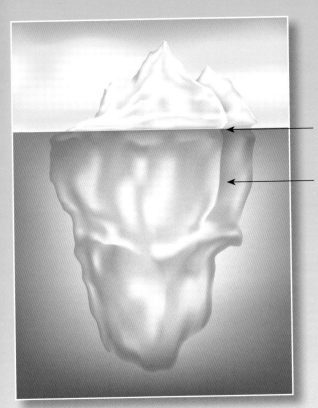

Sea level

Nine-tenths of an iceberg lies below the surface.

Icebergs

An iceberg forms when a large chunk of ice breaks off an ice shelf or a glacier. Icebergs can be a danger to ships. Only a small part of an iceberg shows above the surface – the rest is below.

Did you know?

The biggest iceberg ever seen had a surface area the size of Jamaica! Icebergs can also be up to 150 metres high.

Sinking of the *Titanic*

In 1912, a luxury passenger ship called the *Titanic* hit an iceberg in the North Atlantic Ocean. The ship sank in just under three hours, and 1500 people drowned. The *Titanic*'s owners had claimed it was unsinkable!

Ocean Treasures

All sorts of riches come from the ocean. As well as fish and shellfish, there are valuable minerals, such as oil and gas. Harvesting the ocean's riches, however, is often easier said than done!

Fishing boats

Fishermen set traps and nets to catch fish and shellfish. Different nets are used to catch fish at the surface and on the bottom. Modern fishing boats catch so many fish that some fish are now rare.

Pearls

Pearls are valuable gems made by shellfish called oysters. When a piece of grit gets inside an oyster's shell, a hard, shiny ball, called a pearl, forms around the grit. Diving deep for pearls can be dangerous.

A pearl diver collects oysters from baskets in Thailand.

Oil and gas

Oil and gas are mined from the seabed in shallow waters. A platform called a rig may stand on stilts or may float, anchored to the bottom. Engineers drill into the seabed to reach the oil or gas, and then pump it to the surface.

Salt

People get salt from the oceans by flooding shallow ponds near the sea with seawater. The water dries in the sun, leaving behind the salt.

This salt has been raked into piles.

NORTH CORMORANT

Did you know?

Many modern fishing boats have freezers on board. The fish are frozen soon after being caught to keep them fresh. This allows boats to stay out at sea longer.

WILD WEATHER

Weather is created by the Sun heating the Earth, which makes the air move around. This produces constantly changing conditions, from clear blue skies to gusting winds and deafening thunderstorms. This chapter explains the causes of wild weather, including how hurricanes form and why stormclouds produce hail or lightning. Experts say the weather is getting warmer and wilder. Find out how we can care for the Earth.

Hurricanes

Huge spinning storms with powerful winds are called hurricanes. The winds whirl around a calm 'eye' in the centre. Hurricanes form over warm oceans and do a lot of damage when they hit land.

How do hurricanes form?

As the Sun heats the ocean, warm, moist air rises to form thunderclouds. Cold air rushes in at the bottom. The thunderclouds merge and start to spin.

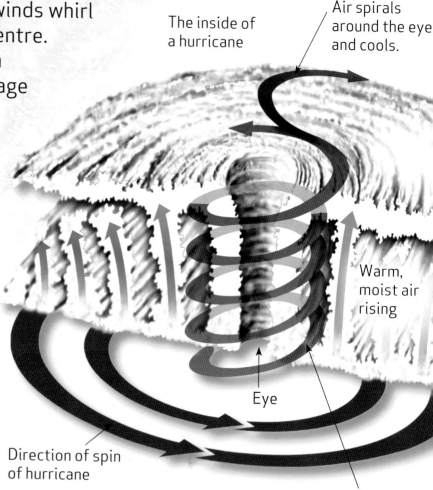

The inside of a hurricane

Air spirals around the eye and cools.

Warm, moist air rising

Eye

Direction of spin of hurricane

Strongest winds are around the eye.

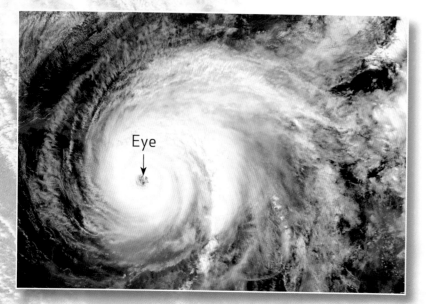

Eye

Whirling clouds

This picture of a hurricane was taken from space. It shows bands of cloud swirling around the eye in the centre. Hurricanes are enormous. They can measure 500 to 800 kilometres across.

Powerful winds

Hurricane winds can blow at more than 300 kilometres per hour. Whole trees can be uprooted. It is very dangerous to be outside in a hurricane.

Did you know?

Fierce storms are called hurricanes if they form in the Atlantic Ocean. If they form in the western Pacific, they are called typhoons.

Hurricane damage

When hurricanes hit land, roaring winds can destroy homes and other buildings. These storms also bring heavy rain and can cause floods.

Hurricane Katrina

In 2005, a powerful hurricane called Hurricane Katrina struck the southern United States. The coastal city of New Orleans was badly flooded. It was the most destructive storm that has ever hit the United States.

Wrecked towns

Hurricane Katrina wrecked seaside towns when it blew in off the ocean. Powerful winds tossed this truck into a tree. Boats were sucked out of the sea and hurled onto the shore.

Rising waters

Roaring winds, rough seas and heavy rain caused flooding. The Mississippi River spilled over high banks called levees that had been built to prevent flooding. Water poured into the nearby city of New Orleans.

Floodwaters burst through a levee.

Katrina facts

 Winds of up to 280 kilometres per hour were recorded during Hurricane Katrina.

 Floodwater covered four-fifths of New Orleans. Homes, shops and parks were covered by up to six metres of water.

Boat rescue

City leaders ordered everyone to leave New Orleans. Helicopters and boats rescued people who had been stranded in their homes by the rising floodwater.

Did you know?

More than 1000 people died during Hurricane Katrina. About one million homes were damaged by the high winds and flooding.

Returning home

When the water finally drained away, the levees were rebuilt. Damaged buildings then had to be repaired. It was a long time before it was safe for people to return to their homes. This family moved back a year later.

Tornadoes

Tornadoes are small
but very violent storms.
A whirling funnel of
air weaves across the
landscape, sucking up debris.

Twisting funnels
can tower up to
200 metres high.

Touchdown!

In hot, sticky weather, warm,
moist air shoots upwards to form
towering thunderclouds. A funnel
of whirling air appears below the
cloud. It forms a tornado when it
touches the ground.

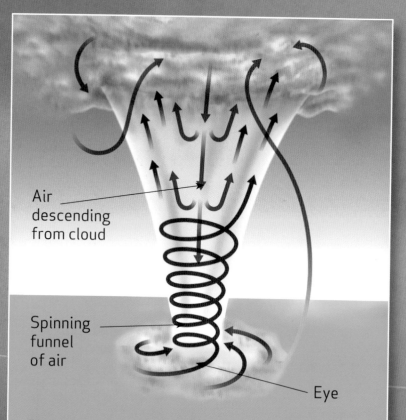

Air
descending
from cloud

Spinning
funnel
of air

Eye

Inside a tornado

Tornadoes are much smaller than hurricanes
– usually less than one kilometre across – but
the winds inside whirl even faster. As in a
hurricane, the winds spiral around a calm
central 'eye'.

Hit by a tornado

The superstrong winds of a tornado have tremendous power. But the path of destruction is usually narrow. A tornado may completely wreck one house but leave the next one untouched.

The damage caused by a tornado in Florida, United States, in 2007.

Did you know?

Winds of about 500 kilometres per hour have been recorded inside tornadoes. These are the fastest winds on the Earth.

The tornado does a lot of damage where it touches the ground.

Tornado Alley

Tornadoes are most common in the United States. Each year, about 1000 tornadoes strike there. Most form in an area called Tornado Alley (coloured yellow on this map of the United States).

Tornado Alley

Gulf of Mexico

CANADA

New York

Michigan

Ohio

Indiana

West Virginia

Illinois

Virginia

UNITED STATES OF AMERICA

Kentucky

North Carolina

Tennessee

Mississippi

Alabama

Georgia

Tornado Damage

Tornadoes travel only a short distance before dying out. But they leave a trail of destruction. Sometimes a whole group of tornadoes forms at once. This is called a tornado outbreak.

Tornado outbreak

In 1974, a total of 148 tornadoes formed in a single day. The funnels swept across 13 US states, as shown on the map. They killed more than 300 people and left a path of devastation 4000 kilometres long!

Tornado shelters

When a tornado strikes, the safest place to be is underground. Many homes in the United States have underground shelters in basements and cellars. People hide if they are told a tornado is due and come out when the danger has passed.

Freak damage

The funnel of a tornado acts like a giant vacuum cleaner. It can suck roofs off houses and flatten buildings. It can pick up cars like toys and toss them into the air.

Did you know?

Tornadoes have been known to pick up very heavy objects. In 1931, a tornado lifted a train weighing 80 tonnes, whirled it through the air and threw it into a ditch.

Storm chasers

Most people will do anything to avoid a tornado. But experts called storm chasers enjoy watching tornadoes up close. When a tornado is reported, they race to the scene to photograph the storm.

Freak Storms

Hurricanes and tornadoes are not the only spinning storms. Whirlwinds can form over the sea or whip up sand in deserts. These storms are usually small but scary.

Cloud of sand picked up by a dust devil

Dust devils

Small tornadoes that form in deserts are called dust devils. The swirling air picks up sand and carries it up to 30 metres in the air. Despite their name, dust devils don't usually do much harm.

Waterspouts

When a tornado strikes at sea, it forms a waterspout. The narrow, twisting funnel sucks up water and sometimes fish too. If the waterspout moves on to the land, it may dump a shower of fish!

Funnel of whirling clouds hits the sea.

Shower of frogs!

Over the centuries, there have been many reports of animals or strange objects dropped by whirlwinds. In 1939, a shower of little frogs fell on a town in western England. Swirling winds had sucked the young frogs out of ponds.

Sandstorms

High winds can whip up sandstorms in deserts. Stinging sand fills the air, and people run for shelter. Wind can carry sand for thousands of kilometres and then dump it far away.

Did you know?

In 1940, a shower of silver coins fell on the Russian town of Gorky. A whirlwind had carried off a hidden treasure chest, which then burst open, scattering coins.

A sandstorm in Pakistan has turned the sky orange.

Thunderstorms

About 2000 thunderstorms rage somewhere on the Earth every minute. These storms can cause terrible damage. They usually happen in hot weather, when warm, moist air rises to form thunderclouds.

What is lightning?

Swirling air in thunderclouds makes raindrops rub together. This produces tiny electric charges. Positive charges build up at the top of the cloud; negative charges build up at the bottom. Lightning sparks between the two.

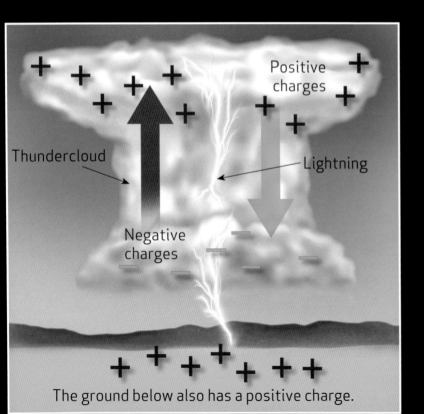

Positive charges

Thundercloud

Lightning

Negative charges

The ground below also has a positive charge.

Static electricity

The type of electricity that builds up inside thunderclouds is called static electricity. This is the same kind of electricity that makes your hair stand on end if you brush it hard!

Thunderclap

As lightning streaks through the sky, it heats the air to incredibly hot temperatures. The air explodes, causing a deafening crack of thunder. Light travels faster than sound, so you see the lightning before you hear the thunder.

Did you know?

The sound of thunder takes three seconds to travel one kilometre. You can tell how far away a storm is by counting the seconds between the lightning and thunder and dividing the number by three.

Forest fires

Lightning can start forest fires, especially in dry weather. In 1988, fires caused by lightning raged through Yellowstone National Park in the United States. Many thousands of hectares of forest were burned.

Streaks of Lightning

Lightning is a huge spark of electricity. It can take different forms, depending on whether the spark flashes between clouds in the sky or shoots from a cloud to the ground below.

Sheet lightning

When lightning flashes between clouds, it produces sheet lightning. The sparks light up the clouds from inside, so they glow (as above).

Forked lightning hits a town in Utah, United States.

Forked lightning

When lightning leaping downwards splits into many branches, it is called forked lightning. Lightning flashes downwards because the ground below has developed a positive charge.

Lightning strike

Lightning always takes the fastest route to the ground. Sparks are attracted to tall objects, such as trees and high buildings. For this reason, people should never shelter under a tree in a storm.

Lightning hits the lightning rod on a tall building in Shanghai, China.

Lightning rods

Tall buildings are often struck by lightning. A lightning rod makes the building safer. Lighting strikes the rod and then runs safely down a wire into the ground.

Monsoons and Floods

In some parts of the world, winds called monsoons change direction in different seasons. Summer monsoons bring heavy rain, which can cause flooding.

Summer rain

Farmers rely on the monsoons to water their crops in summer. These farmers in India are planting rice during the monsoon rains.

Changing winds

This diagram shows how monsoon rains in Asia change direction. In winter, winds blowing south from the mainland bring dry weather. In summer, winds blowing north off the ocean bring heavy rain.

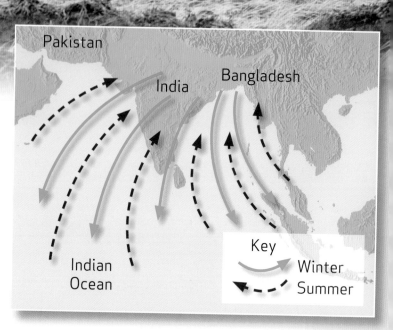

Pakistan

India

Bangladesh

Indian Ocean

Key
Winter
Summer

Hit by floods

Monsoon rains often cause floods in Bangladesh, a low-lying country next to India. Water flooded this village in Bangladesh after a heavy monsoon in 2007.

Did you know?

In 1900, the port of Galveston in the southern United States was wrecked by floods during a hurricane. A wall of water swept right over the town as the hurricane hit.

Storm surges

As a hurricane moves over the sea, it sucks up water. The mound of water, called a storm surge, causes flooding when it hits the coast.

Floodwater covered this US coastal town following a hurricane in 2003.

Snow and Frost

In many parts of the world, winter brings frost, ice and snow. If you wrap up warm, this wild weather can be a lot of fun!

Snow

Snow forms in clouds where the air is below freezing. The moisture in the clouds turns into ice crystals, which join to make snowflakes.

Snowflakes

All snowflakes have six points or six sides. No two flakes are the same shape. A scientist studied snowflakes for 50 years without ever finding two that were exactly alike!

Snow is good for going sledging.

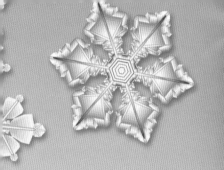

Frost

In freezing weather, ice crystals form on leaves, windows and other cold surfaces. We call these crystals frost. Thick frost can look like a coating of snow.

Icicles

Icicles may hang from roofs, trees and cliffs in cold weather. They form when water starts to drip and then freezes. As more water trickles down and freezes, the icicles grow longer and longer.

Did you know?

Paradise in Mount Rainier National Park, United States, is one of the world's snowiest places. One year, almost 30 metres of snow fell there.

Hail and Blizzards

Extreme winter weather can be dangerous.
When heavy snow combines with strong winds,
we call it a blizzard. Hail is when pellets of ice
fall from the clouds.

Drivers cannot see
far in a blizzard,
which makes
driving dangerous.

Snowstorms

Swirling snow fills the air during a blizzard,
and a layer of ice makes roads slippery.
Roads can be blocked by the heavy snow.

The plough blade pushes
the snow out of the way.

How hail forms

Hailstones form when winds toss ice crystals up and down inside cold clouds. As the ice crystals rise and fall, more layers of ice are added, forming pellets of ice called hailstones. These hailstones eventually get so heavy they fall to the ground.

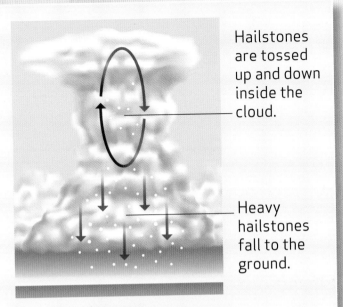

Hailstones are tossed up and down inside the cloud.

Heavy hailstones fall to the ground.

Did you know?

The largest hailstone ever recorded fell on Vivian, South Dakota, United States in 2010. The giant lump of ice measured 20 centimetres.

Most hailstones are about the size of a pea, but some can be much bigger.

Hail damage

Large hailstones do a lot of damage. Hailstones the size of baseballs can dent car roofs and smash windscreens. They can also flatten crops.

Clearing snow

This snowplough is clearing a snowy road. Snow piles up on rooftops and branches during a blizzard. Trees, roofs and even power lines can collapse under the weight of snow or ice.

Changing Weather

In recent years, wild weather has become much more common. Experts say this is because the world is getting warmer and that harmful waste called pollution is to blame.

Greenhouse gases

Gases in the atmosphere trap some of the Sun's heat. They act like the glass in a greenhouse, so they are called greenhouse gases. Pollution is adding more of these gases to the air and this is making the Earth heat up.

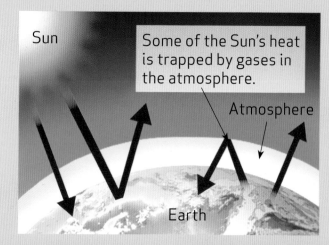

Sun

Some of the Sun's heat is trapped by gases in the atmosphere.

Atmosphere

Earth

Global warming

Power stations burn coal, oil and gas to provide energy. But they also release waste gases into the air. These gases are making the Earth heat up. This is called global warming.

City pollution

Cars give off greenhouse gases. The air in cities is polluted by fumes from cars and factories. Cities cause a lot of pollution because so many people live there.

Cars pump waste gas into the city air in Shanghai, China.

Did you know?

Temperatures rose by 0.5 degrees Celsius during the 20th century. Experts believe the Earth may start to heat up more quickly if we don't reduce pollution now.

Melting ice sheets

Global warming is melting the ice in the polar regions. Melted ice is adding to the water in the oceans, making sea levels rise. This polar bear will have nowhere to hunt if all the ice melts.

Waves could flood this island in the Indian Ocean if sea levels rise.

Caring for our Earth

Global warming is making sea levels rise. It is also causing more wild weather. We need to find ways of reducing the pollution that is making the Earth heat up.

Rising seas

If sea levels carry on rising, cities by the coast could flood. Beautiful islands like this could disappear altogether. We need to produce less pollution to stop this happening.

Cycling

Car journeys cause a lot of pollution. We can produce far less pollution by choosing different ways to travel. People should try to walk, cycle or take the train or bus to work or school.

Recycling

Waste paper, glass, metal and plastic can be collected and sent to factories to be made into new materials. This is called recycling and helps to save energy.

A box of waste ready to be recycled

Saving energy

Power stations that provide us with electricity are adding to global warming. We can help by using energy more carefully. People should switch off lights, TVs and computers when they are not using them.

Did you know?

Energy from the wind, Sun and flowing water can be used to make electricity without causing pollution. These forms of energy are kind to the Earth.

INDEX

Acknowledgments

Artwork supplied through the Art Agency by artists including Peter Bull and Myke Taylor. *Tyrannosaurus Rex* on p26 supplied by Jon Hughes and Russell Gooday.

Photo credits:
b = bottom, t = top, r = right, l = left, m = middle

Cover images:
Front: all images sourced from Shutterstock and iStock apart from pyramids: Getty Images/Richard Nowitz, lovebird: Getty Images/Gail Shumway
Back: bl Getty Images/loops7, br Getty Images/Avatarmin, tl Shutterstock

1Digital Vision,2–3iStockphoto.com/JanWill, 4–5Dreamstime/EugeneBarzakovsky,6tlDreamstime.com/BorisPamikov,6mlDreamstime.com/DmytroKorolov,6bl Dreamstime.com/Htuller,6–7tDreamstime.com/Yakobchuk,6–7mDreamstime.com/WolfgangAmri,6–7biStockphoto.com/AndrewMartin,7tl&blDreamstime.com/ GennadijKurilin,7trDreamstime.com/StephenMcsweeny,7mrDreamstime.com/JoseFuente,7briStockphoto.com/SergeyDubrovskiy,8–9DigitalVision,10–11mNASA, 10 bl Dreamstime.com/Jinyoung Lee, 11tr Digital Vision, 11br iStockphoto.com/Soubrette, 12bl Dreamstime.com/Jeecis, 13tr Dreamstime.com/Ben Goode, 13br Dreamstime.com/StephenMcsweeny,15tlDreamstime.com/JeanneHatch,15mrCorbis/BerndObermann,15mlrDreamstime.com/Geopappas,15brDreamstime.com/ Koskins39,16tDigitalVision,17tCorbis/NawangSherpa/Bogati/ZUMA,17bDreamstime.com/ElenaElisseeva,18–19mDreamstime.com/SonyaEtchison,19bDreamstime. com/Irochka,20–21NASA/JPL-Caltech,21tCorbis/BryanAllen,21bDigitalVision,22tDreamstime.com/IvanCholakov,22biStockphoto.com/zbindere,23bDreamstime. com/AnthonyHall,24Dreamstime.com/MarkBond,25tDreamstime.com/IsmaelMontero,25bDreamstime.com/KunJiang,27tCorbis/JamesL.Amos,28iStockphoto. com/Brett Hillyard, 29t Dreamstime.com/Joe Gough, 29b Dreamstime.com/Andrew Chambers, 31t Dreamstime.com/Musat Christian, 31b Dreamstime.com, 32b Dreamstime.com/DouglasHall,33trDreamstime.com/JörgJahn,33bDreamstime.com/DmytroKorolov,34tDreamstime.com/LaurinRinder,34bDreamstime.com/Nikhil Gangavane,35tDreamstime.comDennisSabo,35bDreamstime.com/DennisSabo,36tDreamstime.com/Maxfx,36bDreamstime.com/RomanKrochuk,37tDreamstime.com/ AnthonyHathaway,37bDreamstime.com/JanMartinWill,38–39Corbis/HerbertSpichtinger,40tDreamstime.com/SebastianKaulitzki,40bDreamstime.com,41tCorbis/ TedSpiegel,42tDreamstime.com/AnatolyTiplyashin,42bDreamstime.com/CharlesTaylor,43lDreamstime.com/PeterClark,43rDreamstime.com/StephenFinn,44t Dreamstime.com/David Lloyd, 44b Corbis/Robert Gill, 45t Dreamstime.com/Daniel Haller, 45b Dreamstime.com/Don Mace, 46t Dreamstime.com/David Lloyd, 46b iStockphoto.com/CarmenMartinezBanús,47rDreamstime.com/RafaelLaguillo,47mDreamstime.com/AndyButler,47bDreamstime.com/PavelLosevsky,48tDreamstime. com/Pancaketom,48bDreamstime.com/Jesse,49tDreamstime.com/Alexkalina,49bDreamstime.com/Aravindteki,50Dreamstime.com/AlenaYakusheva,51tDreamstime. com/RobertCocquyt,51mDreamstime.com/VladTurchenko,51bDreamstime.com/DavidWatkins,52lDreamstime.com/MaximMalevich,52rDreamstime.com/Kameel4u, 53tDreamstime.com/JerryHorn,53biStockphoto.com/PiotrPrzeszlo,54tlCorbis/VisualsUnlimited,54trDreamstime.com/Andreasg,54bDreamstime.com/KirillBodrov, 55tCorbis/Bettmann,55bDreamstime.com/OlegFedorenko,56lCorbis/KarenMichelmore,56rDreamstime.com/YeLiew,57tDreamstime.com/PiotrMajka,57mCorbis/ PaulA.Souders,57bCorbis/JonathanBlair,58tDreamstime.com/MaratHasanov,59tDigitalVision,59blDreamstime.com/NicoleWaring,59bmDreamstime.com/Evgeny Terentyev, 59br Dreamstime.com/Paul Butchard, 60l Dreamstime.com/Htuller, 61t Dreamstime.com/Alexandr Klochov, 61b iStockphoto.com/Donna Coleman, 62t Dreamstime.com/PavelGribkov,62bDreamstime.com/PhilMorley,63tDreamstime.com/NikhilGangavane,63bDreamstime.com/AlenaYakusheva,64bDreamstime.com/ Sugarfree.sk,65tDreamstime.com/MarcoRegalia,65bCorbis/MichaelS.Yamashita,66bUSGS/DavidWieprecht,67tCorbis/JimSugar,67bUSGS,68–69iStockphoto.com/ LizLeyden,68tOAR/NationalUnderseaResearchProgram(NURP),68bDreamstime.com/SimonGurney,69tDreamstime.com/KeoniDibelka,70tUSGS/JimNieland,70b Corbis/GaryBraasch,71tUSGS/LynTopinka,71bDreamstime.com/SamuelPrice,72Dreamstime.com/RobertPaulVanBeets,73tCorbis/MarkDowney/LucidImages,73b Corbis/TWPhoto,74tNOAA/NGDC(NationalGeophysicalDataCenter),74bCorbis/GeorgeHall,75tCorbis/BernardBisson/Sygma,75bNGDC(NationalGeophysicalData Center),76–77tDigitalVision,76–77biStockphoto.com/CKLai,77trCorbis,78–79iStockphoto.com/VernonWiley,80tCorbis/GalenRowell,81biStockphoto.com/Ogen Perry,82Dreamstime.com/MarcJohnson,83tDreamstime.com/KevinWalsh,83biStockphoto.com/WarwickLister-Kaye,84–85Dreamstime.com/SaschaBurkard,85b Corbis/Skyscan,86tDreamstime.com/JoseFuente,86bCorbis/RobertHolmes,87tiStockphoto.com/RobertChurchill,87bDreamstime.com/JasonMaeh,88tDreamstime. com/AlessandroBolis,88bDreamstime.com/AndrewMillard,89tDreamstime.com/RobynMackenzie,89biStockphoto.com/AndrewMartin,90tiStockphoto.com/Danny Warren, 91t iStockphoto.com/Marcella Francescangeli, 91b Dreamstime.com/Joeshmo, 92–93 Dreamstime.com/Troy Farr, 92b Dreamstime.com/Joy Prescott, 93b Dreamstime.com/ReinhardTiburzy,94tDreamstime.com/Spunky1234,94biStockphoto.com/ReyRojo,95tiStockphoto.com/MartinMcCarthy,95biStockphoto.com/Bjorn Heller,96tDreamstime.com/StephenGirimont,96bCorbis/Arctic-Images,97bCorbis/JohnathanBlair,98–99DigitalVision,100tiStockphoto.com/HorstPuschmann,101t iStockphoto.com/RomanKrochuk,101biStockphoto.com,102–103Dreamstime.com/LaurinRinder,102tDreamstime.com/LaurieWeed,103tiStockphoto.com/Sandra vomStein,103bCorbis/ArielSkelley,104tiStockphoto.com/RobJamieson,105tiStockphoto.com/MilosMokotar,105biStockphoto.com/GregBrzezinski,106tiStockphoto. com/GreggMack,106biStockphoto.com/RussellGough,107tDreamstime.com/LingXia,108lJeffSchmaltz,MODISRapidResponseTeam,NASA/GSFC,108bWikipedia. org/Uryah,109tiStockphoto.com,109bDreamstime.com/JeffreyBanke,110tDigitalVision,110bUSGS/NationalCenterforEROS/NASALandsatProjectScienceOffice,111t NASA,111bDreamstime.com/GertVrey,112biStockphoto.com,127tiStockphoto.com,113biStockphoto.com,114tCorbis/AnnieGriffithsBelt,115tiStockphoto.com,115b Corbis/FrankLukasseck,116tDreamstime.com/Pierdelune,116bCorbis/AshleyCooper,116–117mDreamstime.com/Jhaviv,117tDreamstime.com/AleksejsJ.,117bCorbis/ PierreVauthey,118–119Dreamstime.com/VladimirKorostyshevskiy,118miStockphoto.com/ChristopherSteer,119tiStockphoto.com/TomGrundy,119miStockphoto. com/IanScott,120tCorbis/HawesAlan/Sygma,120bCorbis/NextPhoto/Sygma,121tiStockphoto.com/GeoffreyHammond,122–123iStockphoto.com/JamesSteidl,124t iStockphoto.com/MichaelBraun,125tiStockphoto.com/NataliaDiakov,125biStockphoto.com/MichaelSteden,126–127Corbis/RickDoyle,127tDreamstime.com/Jesse, 127mDreamstime.com/Elisalocci,128iStockphoto.com,128biStockphoto.com/MichelleReaves,129tDreamstime.com/CarolynePheora,130tEdwardSimkins,130–131 iStockphoto.com/ReyRojo,131tDreamstime.com/NicoSmit,132tNASA,132biStockphoto.com/VeraBogaerts,133tDreamstime.com/WolfgangAmri,133biStockphoto. com/TrinaDenner,134liStockphoto.com/TammyPeluso,135triStockphoto.com/AdrianBaddeley,135mDreamstime.com/AndreaLeone,135bDreamstime.com/IanScott, 136b Corbis/Douglas P. Wiilson/Frank Lane Picture Agency, 137t Corbis/Bob Gomel, 138m iStockphoto.com/Chris Zwaenepoel, 139t Dreamstime.com/Kiminnb, 140t Corbis/RalphWhite,140bOAR/NationalUnderseaResearchProgram(NURP)/WoodsHoleOceanographicInst.,141bCorbis/RalphWhite,142tDreamstime.com/Pete Favelle,142bCorbis/TimDavis,143bCorbis/Bettmann,144tiStockphoto.com/LuisPedrosa,144bCorbis/MichaelFreeman,145tiStockphoto.com/PatriciaHofmeester, 145bDigitalVision,146–147iStockphoto.com/HansF.Meier,148bJacquesDescloitres,MODISRapidResponseTeam,NASA/GSFC,149tCorbis/DanielAguilar/Reuters, 149b Melissa Ann Janssen/FEMA, 150t Marvin Nauman/FEMA, 150b Jocelyn Augustino/FEMA, 151t Bob McMillan/FEMA, 151b Mark Wolfe/FEMA, 152–153 Corbis/Eric Nguyen, 153t Mark Wolfe/FEMA, 154b John Plisich/ FEMA, 155t Andrea Booher/ FEMA, 155b Corbis/Jim Reed, 156–157 iStockphoto.com/Christopher Walker, 156t iStockphoto.com/VladimirKondrachov,157tlDreamstime.com/ErikLam,157triStockphoto.com/AlexeiZaycev,157bCorbis/NadeemKhawer/epa,158biStockphoto.com/ MarkRose,158–159tDigitalVision,159bNationalParkService,160tDreamstime.com/AlexanderZhiltsov,160biStockphoto.com/MichaelMadsen,161tiStockphoto.com/ LarsLentz,161bCorbis/Reuters,162tCorbis/Reuters,163tCorbis,163bCrystalPayton/FEMA,164tDreamstime.com/GennadijKurilin,164–165Dreamstime.com/Kathy Wynn,165tDreamstime.com/AnnaChelnokova,165bDreamstime.com/GeorgyPchemyan,166tiStockphoto.com/SilviaJansen,166biStockphoto.com/RickHinson,167m Corbis/JimReed,168bDigitalVision,169tDreamstime.com/Bertrandb,169biStockphoto.com/JanWill,170tDreamstime.com/KanuSuguro,170biStockphoto.com/Ana Abejon, 171l Dreamstime.com/Showface, 171r Dreamstime.com/Lukasz Fus.